ÈṢÙ AT THE LIBRARY

A Pandemic Dirge

Also by Kọ́lá Túbọ̀sún

POETRY
Edwardsville by Heart

TRANSLATION
Ìgbà Èwe: Translated Poems of Emily R. Grosholz

ESSAYS
In the Shadow of Context (forthcoming)

EDITED (with Noh Anothai, Wendy Call and Oyku Tekten)
Best Literary Translations anthology

CHAPBOOK
Attempted Speech & Other Fatherhood Poems

ÈṢÙ AT THE LIBRARY

& other Poems

Kọ́lá Túbọ̀sún

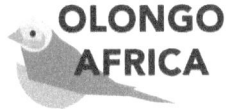
OLONGO AFRICA

This edition is published by OlongoAfrica.com in 2024
www.olongoafrica.com
publisher@olongoafrica.com

Copyright © 2024 by Kọ́lá Túbọ̀sún

First published in Nigeria by Masobe Books. November 2024

All rights reserved.

All rights reserved. No part of this book may be reprinted, reproduced, stored, or utilised in any form, by any electronic, mechanical, or other means, now known or hereafter invented, including printing, photocopying, saving on disk, broadcasting, or recording, or in any information storage or retrieval system, other than for purposes of fair use, without written permission from the publishers.

ISBN: 9798339341109 (Paperback)
ISBN: 9798339342458 (Hardback)

Cover design and internal drawings by Moussa Kone.
All rights reserved. https://www.moussakone.com/

Èṣù

1. "This deity represents the random, unpredictable factor in both divine and temporal affairs. Èṣù is the dialectician of reality, a cautionary spirit who teaches that reality has more facets than one."
   — Wole Ṣóyínká.

2. **"Devil, Demon, Satan"**
   — *A Vocabulary of Yorùbá* (1843) by Samuel Ajayi Crowther

3. "Trickster God of Opportunity, Communication and Instant Messaging"
   — GodChecker.com

Synonyms and homographs: Bara, Exu, Echú, Eshu, Ẹlẹ́gba, Ẹlẹ́gbára, Eleggua, Láaróyè, Lẹ́gba, Legwa

***

"I take the position that the collocation "good and evil" finds no reality interpretation in the indigenous thought system of the Yorùbá, uncontaminated by and through diffusion."
— Ọlásọpé Oyèláràn

"Mr. Kọ́lá Túbọ̀sún, answer me this one question",
a friend asked me once. "Why do the Yorùbá say 'Èṣù má ṣe mí,
ọmọ ẹlòmíì ni o ṣe' (translation: *Èṣù, do not harm me.
Go find someone else's child*) when he is such a 'harmless
just-slightly mischievous' fellow, so useful at helping
us understand the contradictions of our lives?"

My response was in the form of a story I once heard:

*Èṣù, going on a walk one day, decided to confound two friends who had
displayed what he considered an irritating level of public affection for
each other. Wearing an outfit that had two different colours on each side
of his body, one part red and the other black, he approached them. For
some reason, the friends didn't see him until he walked right between
them, so each only saw one colour.*

*As soon as he had disappeared, one friend looked at the
other and wondered, "Why on earth would that red-clothed
man walk between us?"*

*The other answered, equally bewildered, but for a different reason.
"You mean the man in black who just left?"*

*And thus began an argument first on that issue of colour of clothing the
intruder had worn, and then onto other things, until it degenerated into a
full-blown fight, as Èṣù looked on, bemused, at a vantage point.*

*What's the lesson here? Perhaps that you never really know how
friendly you are with someone until you've had a disagreement,
or that if you let a difference in perspectives change who you are,
then you were never close in the first place.*

*It's my understanding that the Yorùbá often wish never to be
subjected to such tests, not because it is always harmful,
but because it can sometimes have unintended consequences.
But as far as Èṣù is concerned, he's just providing one more way to
stress-test what we've agreed upon as conventional truth.*

to Jimoh Isiaq
(October 10, 2020)
and all the Lekki dead
(October 20, 2020)

and to all language warriors everywhere.

Notes on Purpose

That Yorùbá òrìṣà of cause and consequences isn't particularly known for the library, with its silence and awe. Èṣù fit better at a busy crossroads. St. Pancras, maybe, or in some other busy underground station filled with noise, rhythm, and indifference. There, amidst indecisions, misunderstandings, hesitations, he plies his trade.

It was in the fall of 2019 that I encountered the tome where his reputation in the Nigerian cultural imagination had taken its first wild turn. That was Àjàyí Crowther's 1843 *A Vocabulary of Yorùbá*, which was the first time Èṣù was referred to in diabolic terms — devil, satan, demon — something that has proved irreversible through time.[1] I had travelled to London to begin work as a Research Fellow at the British Library under the Chevening Programme, so the meeting was expected. The books had lived in London since publication, coming up for air maybe only a few times a year to curious eyes.

On my daily walks to and from the Library, I contemplated this and other journeys of Yorùbá across the world. Chantelle, my fellow Chevening colleague from Jamaica, helped in the daily exploration of history's serendipities within an old empire. Other times, it was my trip to the Google office at King's Cross nearby that gave a vantage point from which to observe London and

---

1 *"Èṣù" on Google Translate also read "devil" for a very long time, offending millions. When I worked at Google in 2015-2016, I complained and got the translations fixed. But when I left, the changes reverted. Then, in early 2019, I returned to the company in another role and made the changes again, which seem to have stuck. More here: https://x.com/kolatubosun/status/1126419569168519168*

project alternative stories to oblivious strangers traipsing along to their different journeys.

A few months later, the global pandemic began.

Much of the poems in this book come from that travel experience, each bearing some version of the season's instability or the deity's predilection to ambiguity. What started as usual attempts to document an intimate spatial contact turned to a memorial for a time of global significance. Èṣù as an entry-point didn't become clear until the manuscript was almost ready. In October of 2020, after I had returned home, the year wrapped itself in the blood of young protesters at the Lekki Toll Gate in Lagos, mown down by the military while protesting bad governance and the irrational use of state force. As if the pandemic itself was not scourge enough. That #ENDSARS debacle, and the disgrace of state collusion, has already been documented in all its infamy.

The years have gone quickly by but the lessons remain. It's in looking back that clarity emerges. Not always evil; and not always good. Discomfort and confusion, sometimes; but also levity. Like Èṣù locked in a 171-year-old book struggling to escape a fate conditioned by an Anglican preacher, how the memory is deployed determined, in each case, how much of it was lost, and how much was gained. And how much was just another one of Èṣù's colourful outing in the camouflage of a curious season.

It's just poetry, after all. Sometimes, also, just a travelogue, sandwiched between sketches of an artist's brush.

KT
Lagos, Nigeria

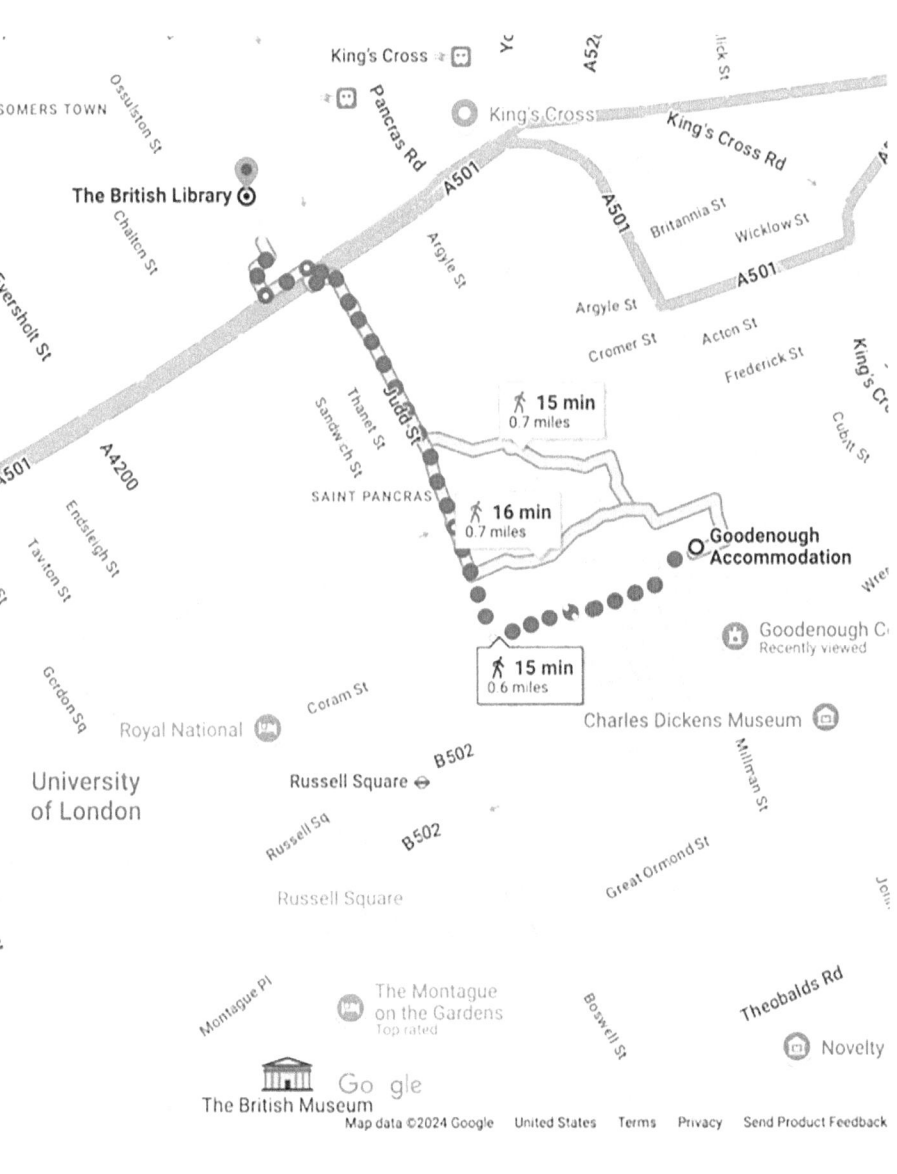

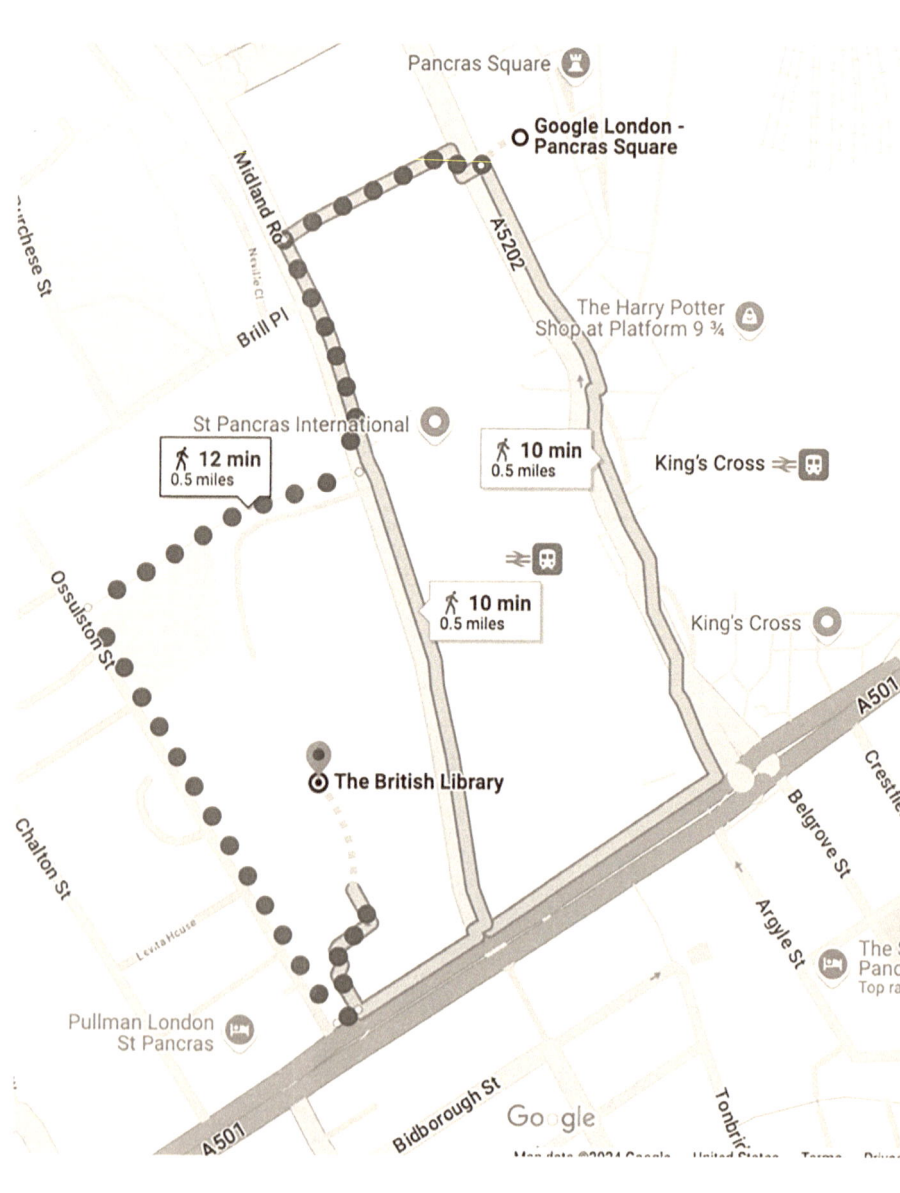

Table of Contents

Notes on Purpose ix

WHITE 1
   Lingua Fracas. 3
   Leg Room. 5
   Airport Pickup 6
   Chat Call 8
   In London The Umbrellas 11
   A Linguist at Primark. 14
   Diet 17
   Witnesses at Peckham 18
   At the British Museum 19
   Deciphering Intentions. 20
   Nelson at Goodenough. 21
   Apple Store, Covent Garden 22
   A Brief Sunshine in Lagos 23
   The Escape 24
   Brit Hunger. 26
   Russell Square Station. 28
   Gone Innocence 29
   Brexit Day 30
   The Books Left Behind. 31
   Crowther's Dilemma 32

BLACK 33
   Èṣù at the Library. 35
   Let Us Pray 38
   The Puke On The Train Floor. 40
   If the Virus Comes to Town 43
   Effluvia 44

The Homeless Are Homeless Still 45
Dystopia 46
Closing Doors 47
In Crowds of Pain 48
The Lines 49
What Next?. 50
Funeral 53
Last Tweets 55
If Only 57
If These Were Written In Times Past 59
Bad Connections 60
Ex-ilé 61
An Empty Town 62
No Rolls at Waitrose 64
Quiet 65

RED **67**
Blood-Spangled Banner 69
Maximum Restraints 70
Soldiers in Lagos 72
Capel Celyn. 73
On New Year's Eve. 75
The Snob 76
To A January 6th Friend. 78
No Wine in my Quarantine 80
London is a Yorùbá Town 83
Home as lights 95

Acknowledgements 97
Appendix. 98
About the Author 100

WHITE

"Time is the deepest wilderness in which we wander."
— Christopher Cokinos

Lingua Fracas

On the plane out of Lagos,
A chatter between strangers
Perked my ears from the discomfort
Of my long tired feet.

"I live in Bristol," the hostess said
To the Nigerian across the aisle,
Both in a moment of shared Britishness
As others settled in.

"My sister lives in Bristol," he answered back
In the same vein and tone, the pride
Of their common homes warming over differences;
Croaky to tiny voice over the heads in-between.

"Nice," she said, strapping in. "It's a nice place."
My boredom feasted on the enthusiasm
Of their bonding talk, and then back
To pre-boarding reality.

"She's a nurse," he said again,
And the crack emerged: A rounded vowel
Where a central one would have fit.
"What?" she asked.
"Naw-se,", enunciating.

I watched the Nigerianism peel away
the practiced years of speech repair;
And there it was, audible to all
Except the one to which it was directed
Who took it for a different word.

"Oh, I live in the *North* too," she shouted back.

Leg Room

Boats were fine.
A fortnight on sea-sickened
Balconies with a view of the continent's
Shore castles of a painful past, at least
Gave leg room for pacing around, and
A view of the birds circling with
The roiling ocean.

Vomits, yes. With hours
For recovery in the bottom of new bottles
Or lovers' bosoms, or strangers' faces,
Gaming the look of spies
From the cold war days — a pandemic
Of its own special kind — under
The view of the heavens.

Not this tube
Taking the path of birds, like Icarus,
Into the breast of the humid sky.
The claustrophobic plop of the ear
In the plane's toilet reminds that speed,
Like the pain in the knee of this dissatisfied
Giant, does not respect the traveller.

Airport Pickup

Through the barricade
Into freedom, the signs beckon
In different fonts: black board,
White chalk. Bold, small, letters.
An iPad once, and a piece of cardboard
On another. Paper and pen
Scrawlings of people whose stories,
Like mine, begins here
In the exhausting end to the long haul.

Mrs Smale on one. Not a typo on 'Small',
I wondered. As with Jonathan Ward,
Clearly someone's son.
Mark Opzoomer will be Jewish
Or not. Oppenheimer twins in name,
From the Feynmann's books, destroyer of worlds.
What he is, for sure, is late.
His driver looks anxiously at the exit.
Mark Hansen, on one. Maybe he's 'handsome'
Or just has large hands.

The one with Krista Goodman was barely
Legible from my distance.
I wondered also
How many of the visitors are spies
Or which had come on a visit

That would find me, in another realm,
Victim to this liberalism of travel.
David Fellows, like a studious dude
Coming for his lover Laura Howie,
On the slate held by the short Asian man.

Joel with no last name is on another.
And Andrew Brown, Mark Whipple, Richard Toby
Near the exit where I was now, staring.

Heading to the subway sign, I saw a familiar one:
Bádé Adébọ̀wálé on an electronic slate.
Welcome brother. The limousine is not yours.
The others waited for Imelda Clifford
And Ms Wells (AGM cars).

Faithful subject of empire, dragging along his pain,
I, with my two bags, will be taking the train.

Chat Call
After Wọlé Sóyínká [2]

The voice seemed reasonable, locution
Impeccable. The young man swore he lived
Close by. Nothing remained
But self-confession. "Sir," She warned,
"I hate a wasted journey—I am big."
Silence. Silenced transmission of
Pressurized good-breeding. Voice, when it came,
Huffy, short minted breath
As a husky radioman. Caught she was foully.
"HOW FAT?" . . . She had not misheard . . . "
ARE YOU CURVY OR RATHER LARGE?"
CTRL, ALT, DEL. Stench
Of rancid sweat drops on electronic bead-mat of log-in chat.
Black paint. Black metal board. Black double-rimmed
PC's glittering screen. It was real! Shamed
By ill-mannered silence, surrender
Pushed dumbfoundment to beg simplification.
Considerate he was, varying the emphasis–
"ARE YOU REALLY BIG? OR JUST CURVY?" Revelation
came.
"You mean—like old or modern Rubensian?"
His assent was clinical, crushing in its light
Impersonality. Rapidly, wave-length adjusted,
She chose. "West African portliness" – and as an afterthought,

---

[2] See: Wole Soyinka's *Telephone Conversation* (1962)

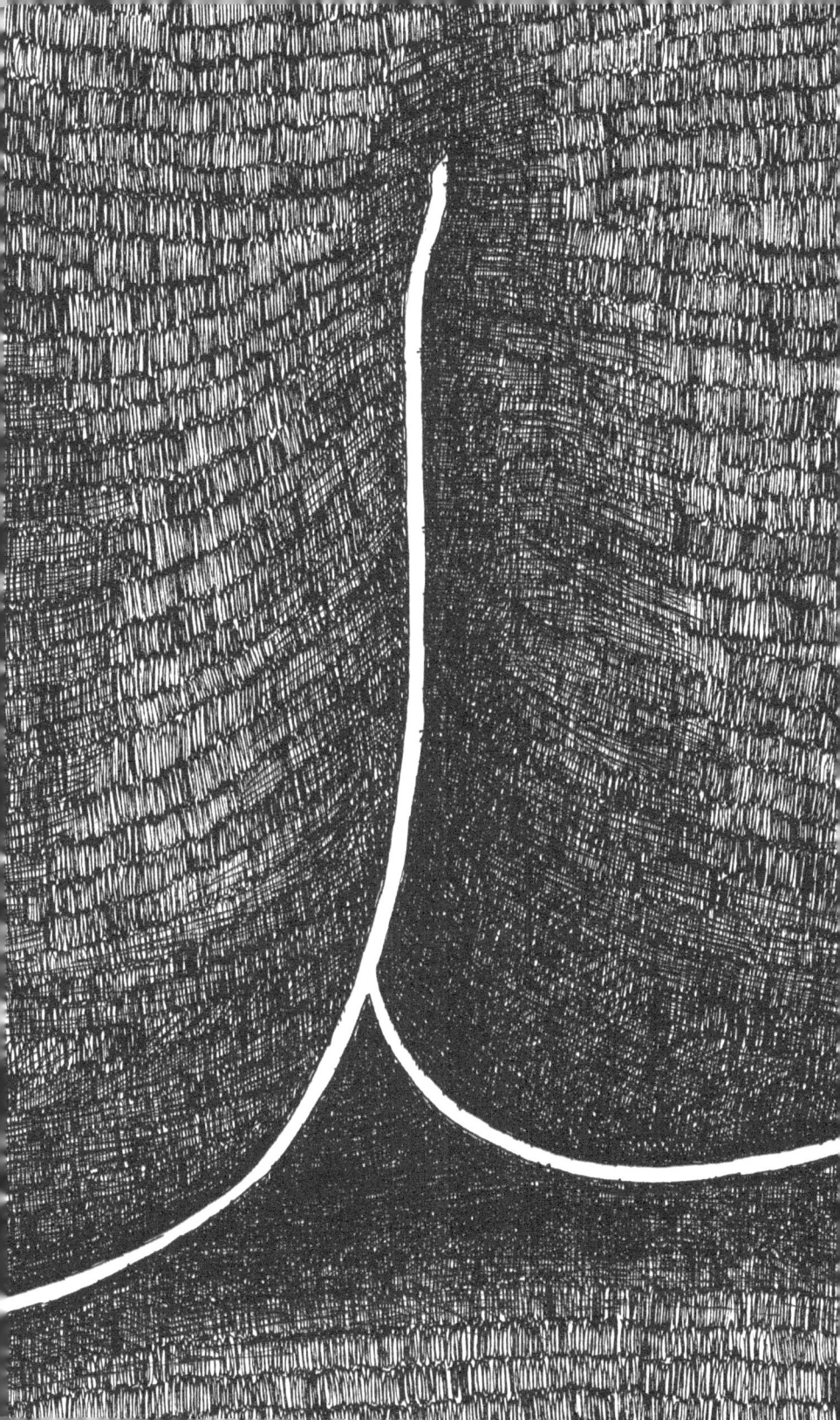

"Down in my profile." Silence for macroscopic
Flight of fancy, till truthfulness clanged his accent
Hard on the microphone. "WHAT'S THAT?" conceding
"DON'T KNOW WHAT THAT IS." "Like chubby."
"THAT'S FAT, ISN'T IT?" "Not altogether.
Facially, I am plump, but, man, you should see
The rest of me. My wrist and ankles
Are merely corpulent. Gravity, caused –
Foolishly, man – by sitting down, has turned
My bottom rotund – One moment, please!"– sensing
His keyboard rasp away like the thunderclap
About her ears–" Come on man," she pleaded, "wouldn't you rather
See for yourself?"

In London The Umbrellas

Like black batons on police hands,
is everywhere, you know,
"Like bread", said the Jamaican,
Dark wet jokes on a rain-soaked night.

Of the long black loaves that held
In purses and swinging hands
At St. Pancras around the station,
We, nervous that the weather
Now clear and bright
Carried some wet animus around
The hidden side of its face
Played in puns with the sliver of sun.

And when, in mere hours
The cheery glow of road tar snaking
From Euston Road sits squelching
Under our antsy boots, or at Chinatown
The tourist mopeds taunt
With fake security in the warmth
Of leather and music, the British
Bread morphs like a winged bat

Out into the sky to give succor
Or style to all but the strangers,
And the guest whose shoes do not fit

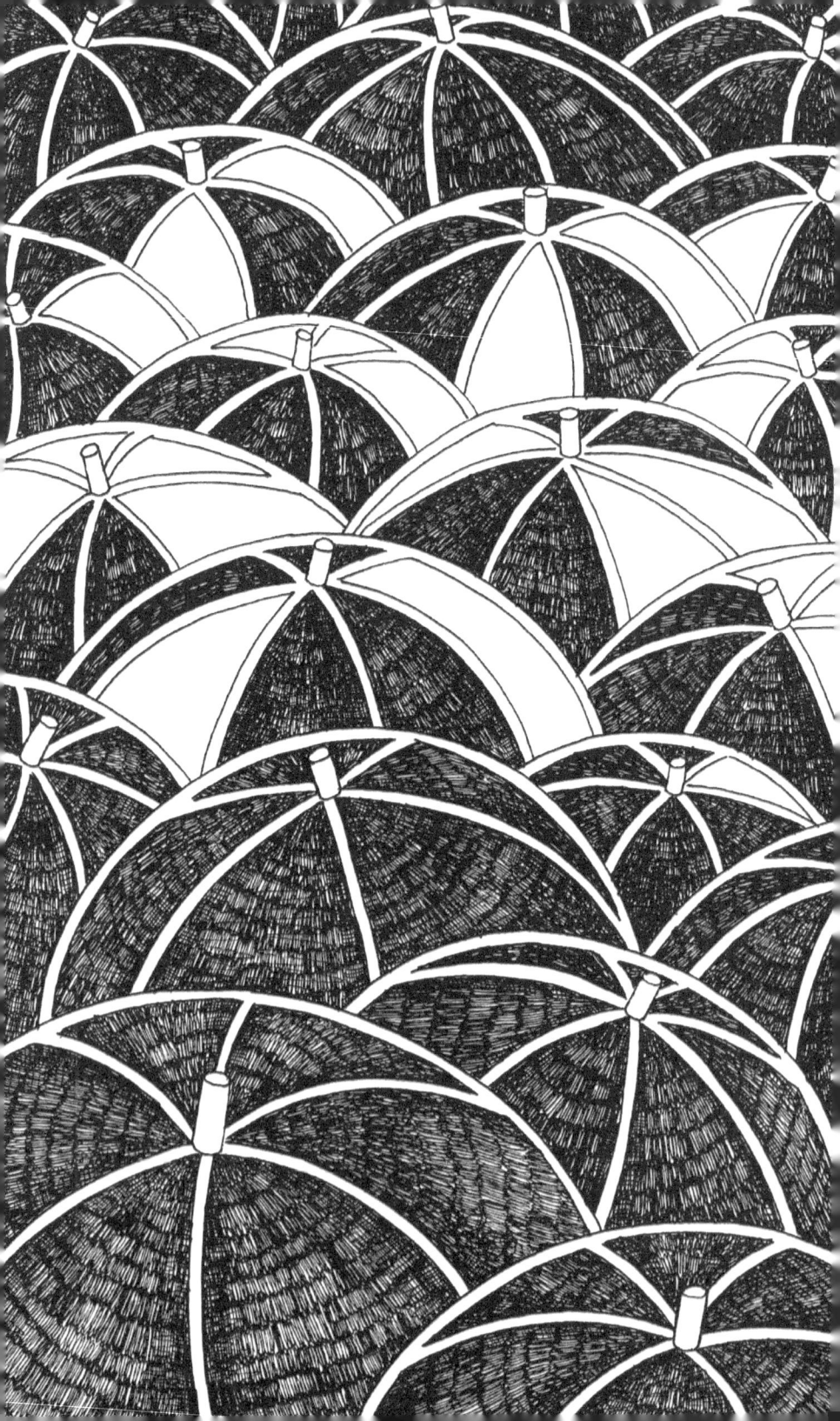

The wetness, whose jacket soaked in
The gods' wet tears, whose cheer
For an àbíkú day is muffled
By the sad weeping night.

A Linguist at Primark

Turkish, perhaps, the hair suggests
Of the man — Black curly beards through
Which the hot pottage words escape
Into the face of his girl staring up at him.
He prattled on, hand on her waist.
Polish perhaps, another one;
Silver hair, copious chest,
Gray sweater and a basket.
But how could the syllables tell?
The payment line curves
Through three seeming aisles, so.
Spanish, certainly, on the phone,
Sizzles like butter through her brisk
Walk past me towards the door.
"There's the changing room owa there",
An Indian, certainly, points someone on,
Rolling the fricatives over his millennial tongue.
There was the one I can't figure
Because the woman is black
Who said it, and the man looks
Russian to whom it is spoken in pain
At the foot of the escalator, bags in hand.
Taiwanese, it seems, a young lady
I could see at the counter ahead,
Lips pursed at the slow customer
In front of the one in front of her.

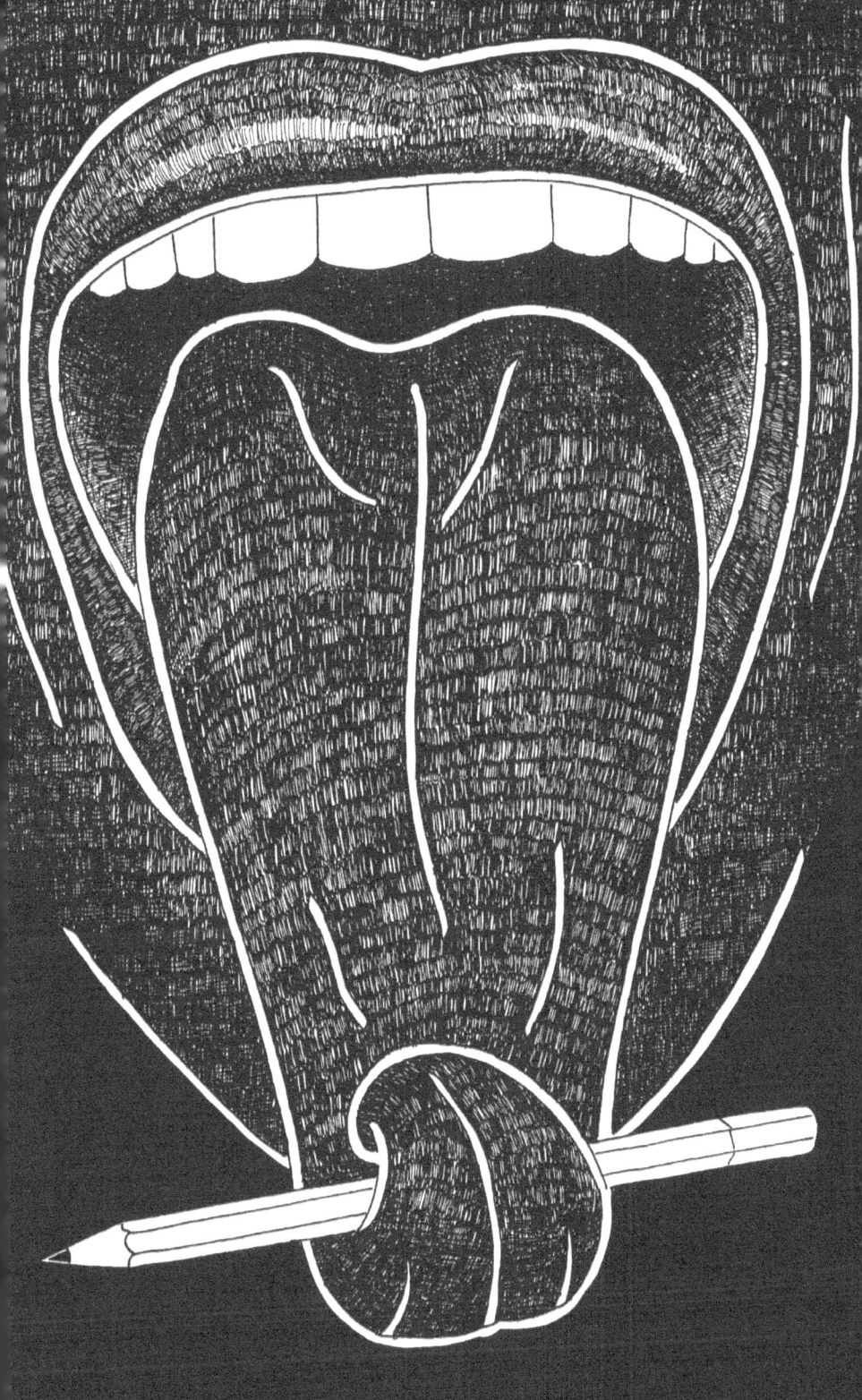

Babyish, the little child of about two.
"Dah. Not Dah," she answers her mother
Who had wondered what she wanted
In the list of snacks on the shelf
Near the payment counter.
"NEEEEXT!" I was called — English, certainly;
In a tired tone from the hours of standing there.

Diet

Cottage Pie at the Library:
Carrot, and mashed potatoes,
With minced meat and salad,
Are a little familiar from times
Spent across the sea.

Another day, it was yellow rice,
Chickpeas, Mushroom, onions,
And tomato sauce, a dish
Likely from Southern Asia,
But here nevertheless on my British plate.

Rhubarb dessert with cream,
I liked, with boiled apples,
and something that tastes like apricots.

Witnesses at Peckham

In the cold, they stood
By the bridge, journals in hand
In Yorùbá, from many aeons past:

Devout to the end
In wraps of shawl and a faith
We only carried on the tongue.

At the British Museum

Empire in columns blank —
A crime scene on Russell Square,

The sturdy eyes of glass around
The halls, the Black guards

Pacing the floors with flashlights
On the hip, with dry smiles offer no hint

Of recognition of our shared dispossession.

I go down to the basement
To pay homage to the Ọba

And family, still locked there in glass
Panes with the leopard, a bronze cockerel,

And the rest of the carved plates
From Britain's last pirate tour.

Deciphering Intentions

At the bank, the Jamaican official who also was kind and patient showed peculiar interest in the meaning of the "fellowship" I had mentioned I was on, and whether I had left the old country job "to come work for the Lord in London" was why I was here, bearing a knapsack of missionary burden in the heart of Empire, and here at the customer's desk behind which many others waited in line conscious of our murmured rapport.
Far from it, I replied, fetching my card from the wallet, to tell how research fellowships worked.
The single mother of a two-year-old, she was — "Jamaican men, you know," she explained as if in practised defence — spoke also of her athletic ambitions.
"My mother works here too," she said again to beg understanding for the new choices that keep her here in a suit on a Monday caring for the needs of strangers needing new accounts to feel among. Easing customer pains with British tongue, with a patience that soon became familiar.
"You must meet beautiful women at the Library then," she said at last, in tone of voice revealing nothing still, nor the face, as I looked for whether a hint of a smile might speak to what was not yet clear.
"Only at the bank," I sputtered back, recovering my initial disbelief at how much I'd lost in the art of flirting.

Nelson at Goodenough

It took the pain of distance
To see what a year away meant
When your eyes, over the screen,
Peered into my present, asking
Questions, restless like the leaves.

In London, the warmth of the room
Beat out the winter blues,
We walked to O'Neils one Sunday
while your mother slept away
The respite from our ruckus.

In three weeks we gathered time
Into the vat of family almost lost,
Where the world's crumbling smile
Beat around the small spaces
Of our now exiled home.

Apple Store, Covent Garden

Monochrome dystopia
Navy blue on black
Apple watches. A half bitten logo
As a nerd nipple across the chest.
The sneakers beneath it all
And rain/cowboy boots
The young lady wore.
Jeans. Blue monochrome
Customer service
With eyes glued on the iPad
That seems to direct them
Everywhere in this stone house
But to where I am
Still waiting to be seen
While efficiency runs a circle
Of robotics round the corner
Of my weary eyes.
"Sorry for keeping you waiting,"
One approached me in the end.
"Can I call you Kal?"

A Brief Sunshine in Lagos

Is gold, dust-fog layered heat-
Welcome, in February, when
The leaves of Camden
Speak in shivers of a coming doom.

Noise and shuffle, the feet
At Ìkejà to Ọbáléndé to Jákàńdè
Car honks that speak no calm
To the history of bewilderment.

Well, family.
The blend of bodies
Save me from the rage of the cold-
Hearted pedestal on which the distance
Builds the core of its allure.

I'll be back soon enough on the hopes
Of spring being a much nicer host
Than the words about this Englishness
Of the coming season also suggest.

The Escape
June 2020

Two astronauts mounted Dragon,
And headed moonwards, away from beleaguered us.
The day the planet burned from years of pain
Or smoke of carbon, or just the noise from a neck
On which a policeman's knee
Rested a racist weight of wasted years.
That day, fire raged across the earth
From voices tired from waiting, heavy from asking,
Cracking from the echoes that Baldwin, Davis, Morrison
Bellowed back from the mind of unending time.
I watched the launch, a white phallus piercing the sky,
With hopes of those to whom the earth is a wasted space
To whom all hope is lost for redemption now.
Except the sweet relief of escape,
The virus, or flesh wound from eager police guns
In Washington or Southern Kaduna, mark their earthly terrain.
That the death racing behind us still
Has, for a moment, let these two go scot-free,
Faced up, back tied tightly to their throbbing seats,
Thrust upwards, frontier men in white
High speed Tesla-aided fleeing out of the firmament
Had me green, waiting for my own true escape.
I wondered too how much of our pestilence
Has gone with them there, and how much will return
Again with the men, now changed by a cosmic scope.

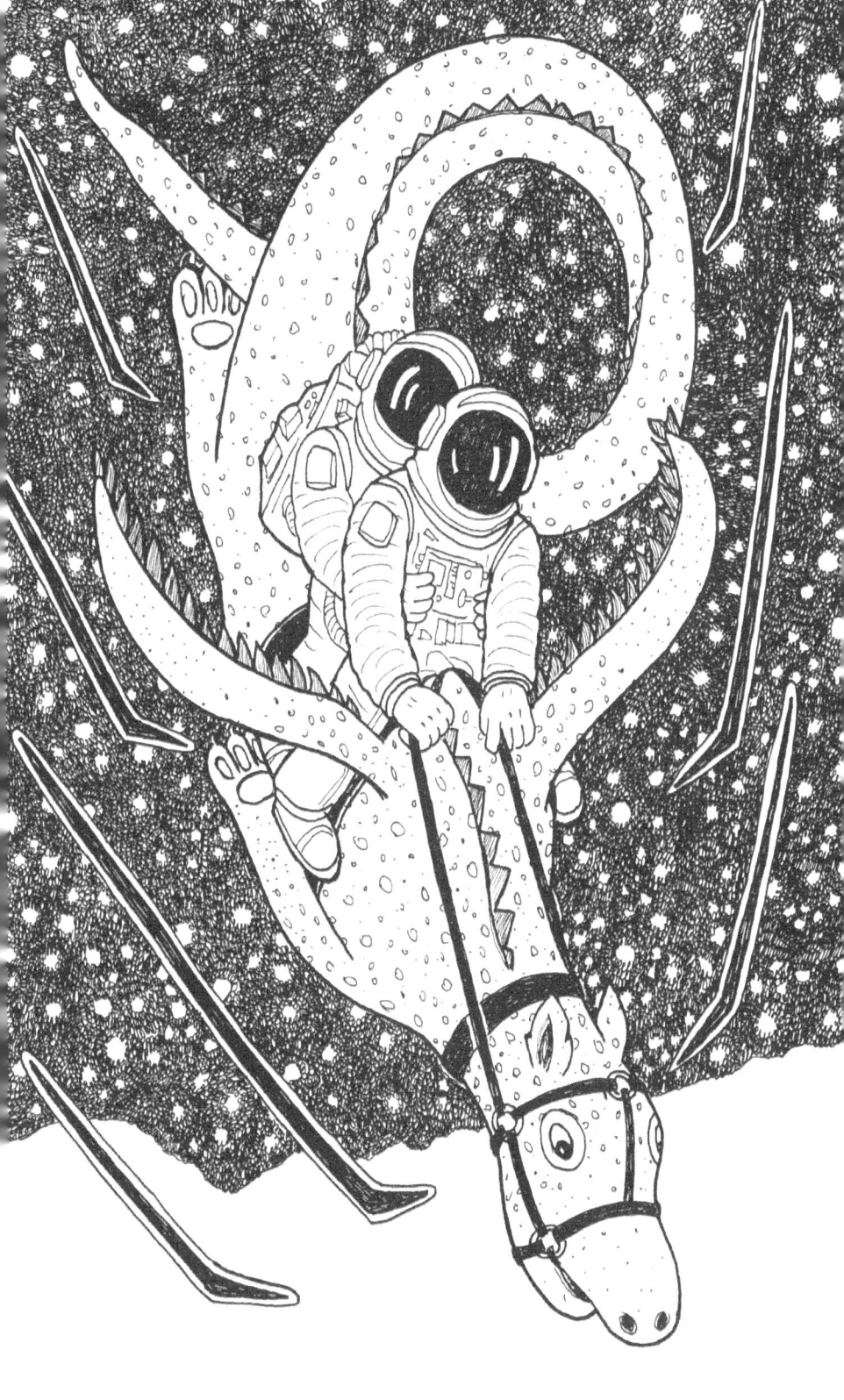

Brit Hunger

Hunger does not know
The difference in the shape
Of the hole in the grey mushroom
On a half English breakfast.
Or the dryness of the sausage at O'Neil's
Compared to others, or the small-sized
Orange juice at Half Cup on Judd St.
The joyless combination of items at lunch
At the British Library cafeteria, upstairs.

The runny yolk of the eggs
Ruin the plate long before the fork
Reaches the mouth with the weight
Of more bumper memories.
Stomach cramps speak their own
Loud language through the night
In rumbles of feelings defying
An English word.

Yesterday, I found another place
To eat, downstairs, at the Library
With a few friends, and quieted
The depth of the gnawing gut
With gulps of gumption. We were
Surrounded by chattering guests.

Hunger does not know the difference
In the shape of my mouth
While I pray gently for spice and known
Tingling in well-spelt menus
Spread in a verbose verse affliction
Missing everything but a satisfying taste.

Russell Square Station

There are 176 steps —
More like a million —
To the surface.

But Èṣù is there
In the concrete throng
Of the Tube's warren

Wiping the meaning clean
Off the clear warning signs.
"Come on, you can walk it;

Just one more step, traveller,"
As tired muscles croaked
Pain within the echoes of the well.

Gone Innocence

Bring the lies of childhood back
The rationales that brought an end
To questions, though spurring a few more.
Bring back the whoppers and fables,
The giant tales with opaque fingers
And the little ones with a luminescent sheen
Like a dancing shadow on the wall.
Bring back the protections that spread
On childhood dreams like guilt blankets
Throttling adventure with fear and a dare.
Bring the end of the world in invisible ropes
Laid to keep our feet from stumbles,
Within established spaces, free from harm,
But only kept the world flat for a season,
More removed like a universe away
Where magic blends with the hint of danger.

Brexit Day

A day at the Library spent
Within books hauled to the head of
Empire years ago by something lesser than love.

Reams of history surround me
And the scent of dry rust
In well preserved loaves of texts and sheet

Binders creak free, fancy spines
Caked by time and storage held firm
By stern rules of item handling:

Beaded snakes for page care, and
Soft foams for back support when open
To read how much the world once meant.

The Books Left Behind

Chitterlings of words
Packed on the shelves
Will stare in silence
At the box room where
I leave them on trips,
Unannounced.

Cleaners will pat them
Down, tasting through
Private notes left in-
Between history's tomes
And serrated morsels
Of contemporary blues.

The gourmand will return
To leftovers, years hence
With a love that may
Or may not be sour;
Dog-eared joy and dread
for a re-united taste.

Crowther's Dilemma[3]

To do or not to solemnly swear
By the logic of one's righteous faith
Which demands something new to fear
In colours of an ageless wraith?

To turn or not to camp one's tent
In scrolls that now prescribe
A culprit for the world's ill intents
In shapes of the native tribe?

To say or not to chant the blessings
On missionary certitude to might
And consequence in the land of kings
Whose mores gave the guests a fright?

To scribble or not to mark for history
Lexicography of imperial thought
In familiar words than the joy of mystery
— the future to their angry lot?

To pray or not to beg the gods
For this one gentle smear.
And let the years that chase the words
Beg for life's tough repair.

---

3   Bishop Samuel Àjàyí Crowther (1809 – 1891), African preacher, missionary, and lexicographer, influenced not just the renaming of the Yorùbá deity after the devil; other records suggest that he did the same with the Igbo deity "Ekwensu" as well, who is now permanently associated with the diabolical.

BLACK

"May the forces of evil become confused
on the way to your house."
— George Carlin

Èṣù at the Library

Long skull man, judge of the junction.
There, at St. Pancras, within the throng
Of texts and men, Bishops who think
That they know you well enough to spell;
We wrangled through history's show and tell
Like the player you are, beating tricks
Into scripture, textbooks, and fiber optics.

Long skull man, wall of concrete stone.
Where I found you was damp — sheave tomes
Of vellum. It was appropriate that we met
There at that time, company in exile.
Seeing I could not set you free while
We stared in space, fingers on the spoils
Of the moment, reeking of kernel oil.

Long skull man, benefactor of the town.
What say you now to the blame your crown
Bears for where we are, fleeing other's warmth
For safety; hiding behind the fabric trance
Like drunk masquerades spent of dance?
Where have your tests led us now, messenger?
How do devout breaths hide from danger?

Long skull man, the named-bearer of whips.
For how long will the welts mark these strips

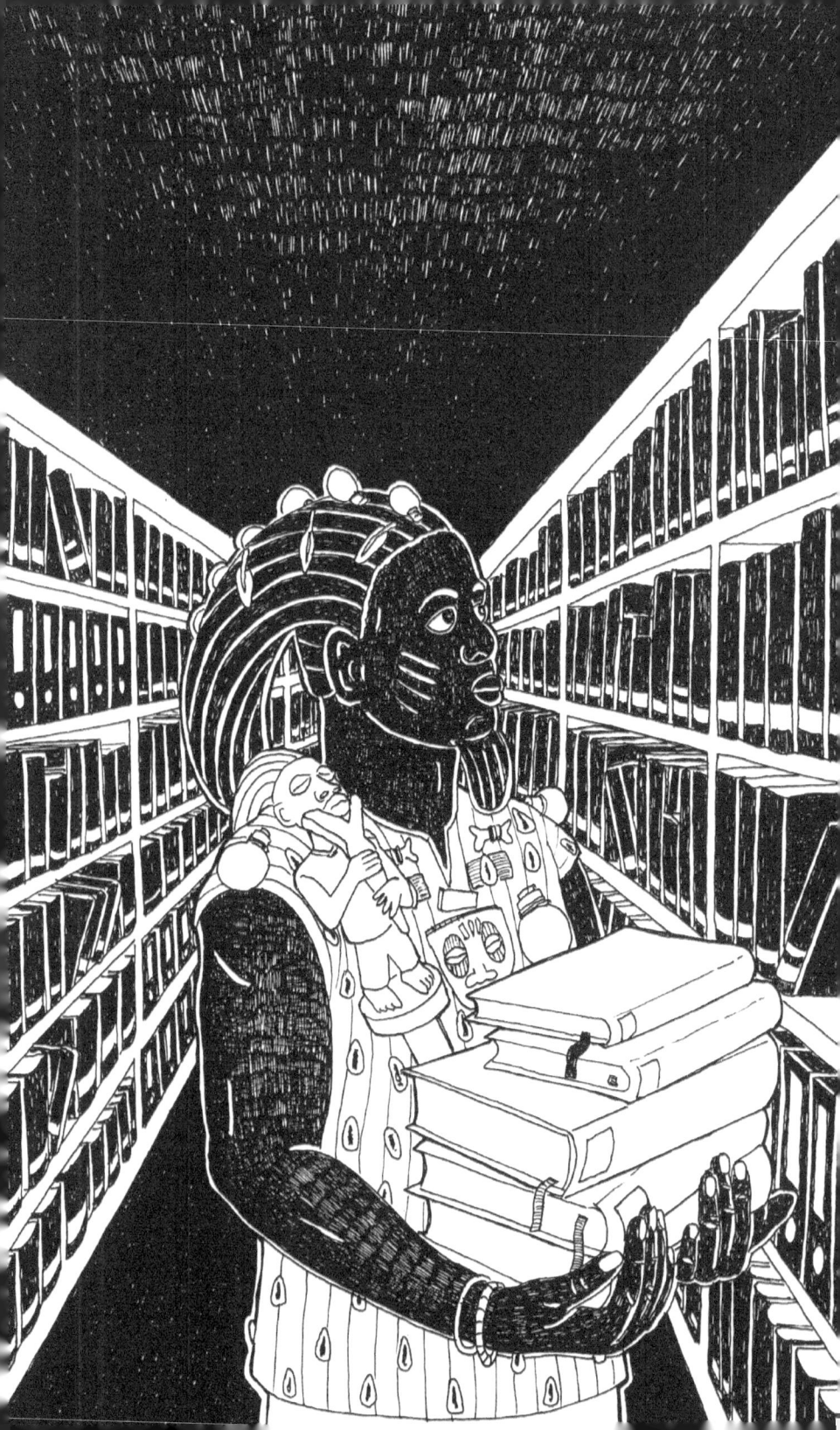

On earth. Early in the year, the lessons have pushed
Our supplicants through the scanty streets to me
Looking for meaning in faces they no longer see.
I have vouched for you away from the ancient texts
So here I surrender to whatever comes next.

Long skull man, streaming tears of blood.
Did you not wash our stains off the flood
Your scribes have swum across the borders of town
Turning friend to foe, word crumbs to meat,
History on its head that children now repeat;
Drum patterns, dialectics, now sweeping through
The season like a spring of poisoned dew?

Let Us Pray

The palms do not deceive,
The Yorùbá say. Drops and torrents
Under the faucet. Or rain. One hand
Rubbing the ills of the world away
From the other. Go, evil go.

A time uncertain, now,
With news chasing another one
Across the world, germs
Turning around the hubris of our fears
Water comes to cleanse the town.
Propitiation to mother's warnings
Before food: wash your hands.

For now, libations to the deities
Of new beginnings, of the herbs,
Of fertility, now giggling in concert —
white — by the Ọṣun River.
Wash us clean, River goddess,
When your wrath at last is done.
Wash us clean.

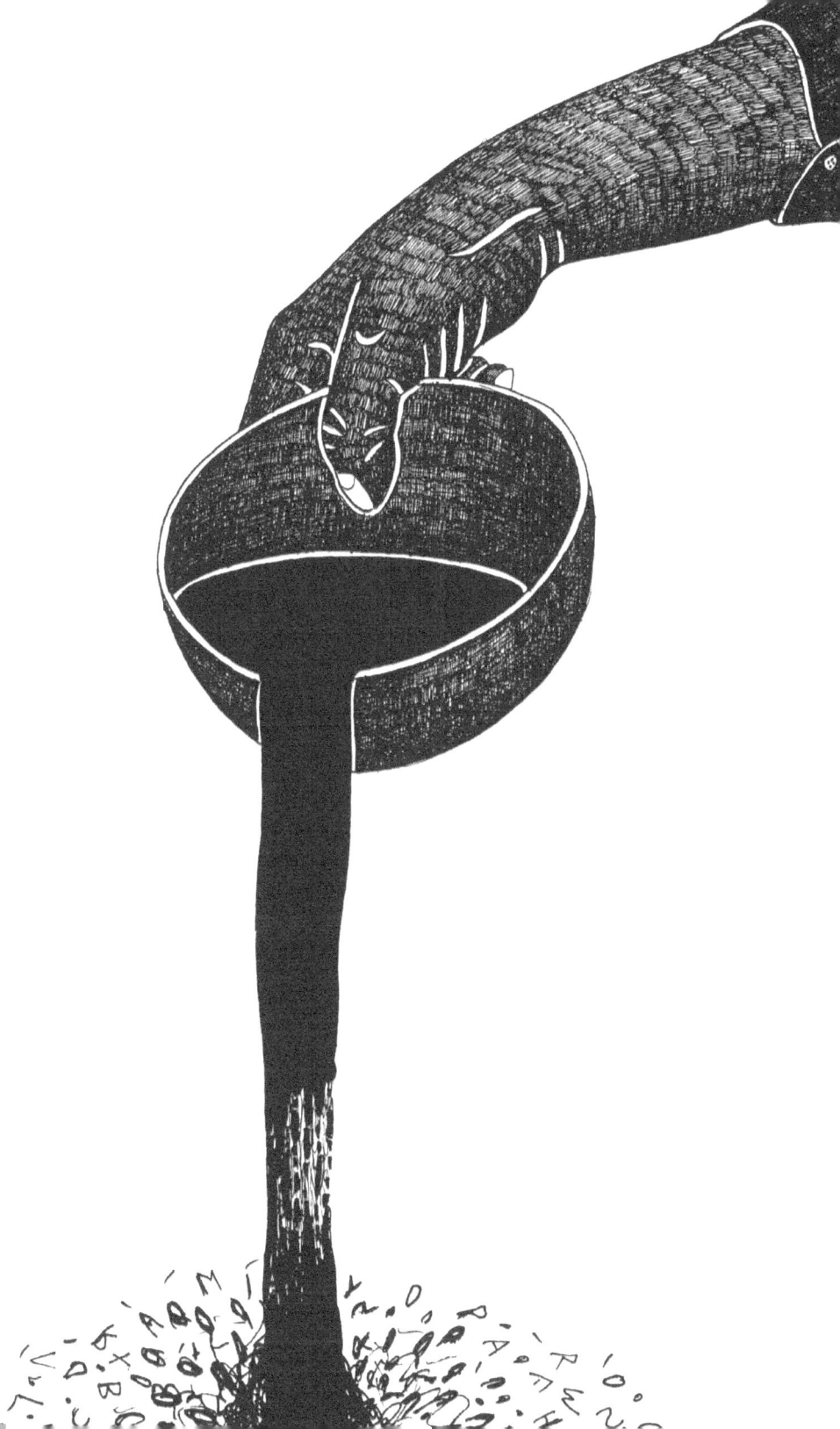

The Puke On The Train Floor

Dawn journeys, the path of food;
Organic or junk or a drink at the pub
The night before, or mummy's special dish,
Vegetarian and gluten-free.
The teenage girl's gut bears travel
For viruses, slugs, the January flu
And all ills from evolutions before
That have found us here, in the train
In the morning cold, stacked like beers.

And there it came, onto the metal floor,
Putrid porridge rain into her mother's shawl
In splatters, and about the train car.
Head bent low, feet parting way for gravity
I saw, through the slit of bodies, the liquid burps
And the foul air from Acton Town to Russell Square,
Her mother's repeated pleas for pardon
In resigned embarrassment.

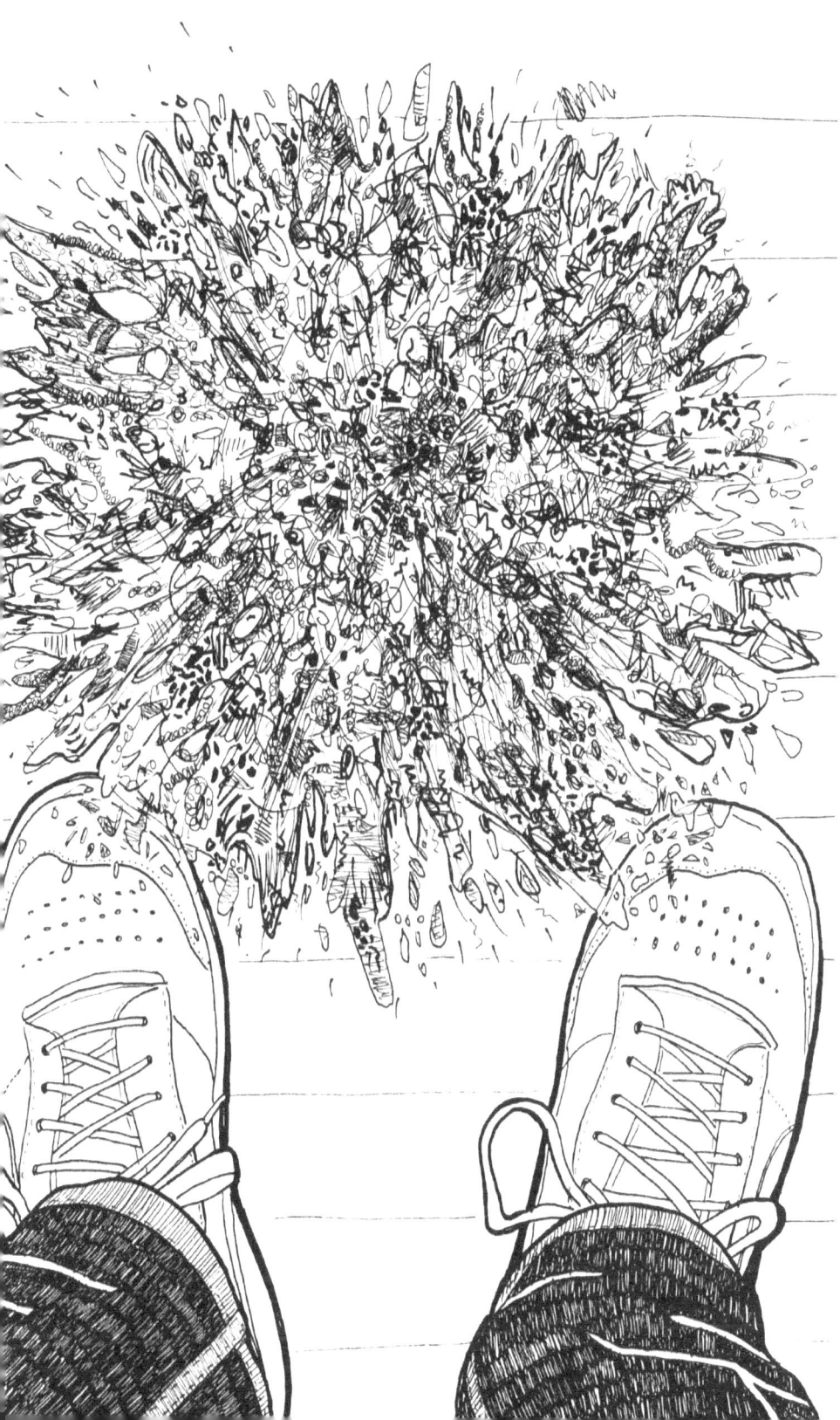

They've left now, the creamish puddle
On the floor for the city's polished shoes
Lay spread like the commonwealth
For brisk steps and posh pained tones
Who come in, briefly, and flee right after,
Holding their noses, back into the waiting crowd.
Long journeys, the path of food — I thought,
Dinner tables, and warm nights, and morning
Trails of bacteria or other ills under shuffles of feet.

If the Virus Comes to Town

It will be via the Oxfordshire route
Via bike and train and car and foot
On dear Nora's daily commute.

My friend the hippie rides through
City to country daily, ferrying goo
And the world's microbes of varying hue,

Backpack of the pestilence in tow.
She coughs aloud and my alarm bells go
Wild with my mother's warnings so:

"Don't touch strangers now, you hear!
I know it is spreading everywhere
Leaving nothing behind, son, but despair."

A piece of wood between us squeak
To nothing but the dread that wreaks
Pain by the sound the seasons speak.

Effluvia

When it rains, at home,
What opens is often more
Than the leaking kegs in the sky
Laughing wet guts on an already beaten town.
The grounds open too —
Clumps from grime-suffused drains
Sweeping throbbing curses of the city's
Angry, hungry, battered shells
To the doorsteps of the profligates
In the seat of power.

Now that the epidemic drizzle
From depths of nature
Has come, invisible, to test the dams
Of our sapien brows, what opens now
Are the seepages of our complacency,
Bile from power show — police
Whipping food sellers in Ìkòyí —
With same old pox on systems
Designed to keep a rot barely seen
Beneath the rags our city wears.

The Homeless Are Homeless Still
March 2020

By the Library, facing the bar across the road
Covered in dirty white wool, head buried
In the concrete corner of the wall,
His leg stuck out at the bottom, facing off
What is left of the world's hysteric misery.

Or her — since one could never tell who
Is in there, or whether it breathes the same
Air that other mortals have, filtered away
With masks and shawls and distancing
In a bid to stay alive. But there she is

Faced-down in the cold morning,
Less bothered by a virus that takes its turn
Just after the winter, the famished gut,
Overdose, strangers on a killing spree,
Ritualists from faraway, and modernity.

Dystopia

Reams of silence are cut in half
By a cough: a virulence in season.
The end of the world is suspended
By the thread of an empty poem.

Underground at Goodenough,
Surrounded by cricket sounds and feet
From nightcrawlers scrounging
What is left of London's sappy soul

I stared into the new future dawning
In the distance, and saw nothing back.
This is how the world ends again, perhaps
a rapture quicker than the bible foretold.

Closing Doors

In-between acceptance and hope
The balance weighs in a faulty middle.
One leg in the cold country, doors
Slowly closing up all exits, all help,
Another in a place where bodies, blood
And dread promises at least the boon
Of heat and bread, leavened in sweat
Beads and song.

In Crowds of Pain

There are the rules against bodily contact
And feet around these wide open places
And words belched so close into each other's face.

As are against murder and hate in the name
Of the law, knee or shoulder or gun or gas;
Spread thin into the face of the gathered mass.

The laws that kept the nation calm over
The years have required compliance, peace,
And safety in the warm arms of rank injustice.

And so, out the rules went, heavy with bricks
That broke into windows in our camera glare
With the wild brew of a people's run out of care.

My heart, remaining in Minnesota under the knee
Of the oppressive state, thumps in Lagos at the many more
Around, in drapes of blood around even our shore.

The virus no more holds sting, even as it grows
To claim its scalps from Brooklyn to Delhi to here
Where the other bile of hate remains a deathly stare.

The Lines

At the shop were at once two, then three
Then one rowdy point when the door opened
So that select people can be let in.

Gloves and masks and sweat and worried
Looks did not stop the familiar melee
Towards the golden door when the time came.

Once every ten minutes, the guard arrived,
Solemn like St. Peters at the judgment gate
Deciding saints and who goes back into torment.

Whose grandma deserved mercy. "Grey hair,
Can't you see?" Or who deserved warning
For being too eager the other time around.

Whose voice rang too loudly, who moved too
Close to the next person on the hand-drawn line
That now must tell us when it is time to eat.

What Next?

Will the earth heal
For a moment
While the trains are paused
And the noise from the rattling
Creaks of wheels on rails
In the underground cease
Enough for the rodents
To return to play
Freely on the crumbs
That will stay longer than
A few days on the curbs?

Will the sky breathe?
The contrails are gone too,
With the sonic scars
That took us, years after years,
Through cumulus and rain
Through bubbles of nature's
Foul breath we continued
To sour with oil fumes
And greed, speed and a million
Restless reasons,
Bags and dreams in hand.

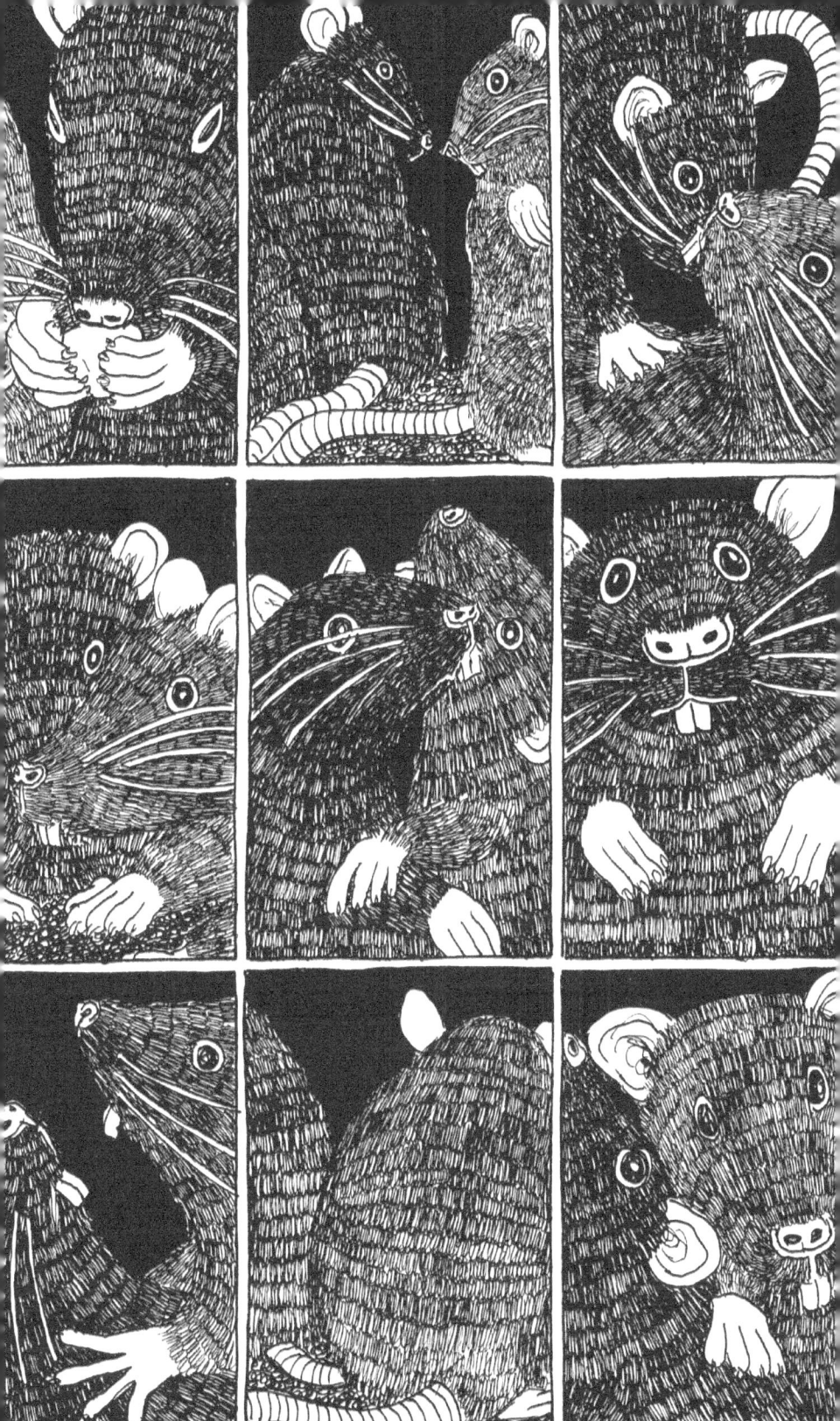

Will the gods return now
From war, now back on the board
Of their evening games,
To rinse the soil of the stench
Of the bile on which the seeds
Of our memories have grown
Tall like a fevered dream?
Will the seasons return
The soft petals of succour
When the rage of our feet
Have left the ridges of the farm?

Funeral

My coffin, when I go, will be long:
Oakwood, ìrókò, cedar-carved, a song;
Fine crafted ant food, weevils bait
In cubic metres, a giant ode to fate
And frailty in a heap of human dust.

The bottom will be cut for my feet
Like Múyì, our friend who lay discrete
Now at Sángo, last seen heading in
Without shoes -- he wasn't needing it
Amidst the dirge of the college crowd.

And the soil will be soft with the tears
Or spittle, or the warm piss of years
Layered upon grains of waiting earth
Worm-fertilized and baked in the sun
Waiting for the bale of my cold flesh.

Seed for trees for which the soil
Had waited all along; life-sized toil
In fancy wear, chosen in air-conditioned
Shops in the city, a special for the departed
Son who must not be seen in yesterday's
Clothes. A decent farewell to rust.

Not having chosen where to sleep — forg
etfulness caused — the weight of my log
on the shoulders of pallbearers will deserve
the relief of descent into where all seeds go
in renewal commune with the flowers of spring.

Last Tweets
For Pius Adésanmí

Òkú ń sunkún òkú
Akásoléri ń sunkún ara won

Because we do not know
which is the last collection
we'd take from the public
cooperative, or the last piece
of clothing, freshly sewn,
that will remain unused on our
shelves when we step out
into the cold morning air
and into the arms of waiting
history, we say our goodbyes
in every tweet, every like, every
wave and thumbs thrown
into conversations never concluded,
projects never finalized, meetings
never actualized over distances
drawn by fate and time.

Because we do not hear
the farewells in the laughters
drawn on our quotidian chores,
the pain filtered through every visa
wait, and security check and pat downs

through Ethiopia and Istanbul and
Heathrow and Paris; and in the
shrugs we substitute for commentary
when the weight of circumstances
push us into the hammock of curated silence,
we settle for hugs and bubbles
of thought in each other's' way
when their face flies into our view
on a quiet night, when the last
thing we wanted to hear was
"Didn't I see him just last…"

Because we do not know
on whose head the sequined cap
that finally caught up with Aríkúyẹrí
will land next, in the weight
of its inevitability, drawn from
close shaves, miracle saves,
mothers' prayers, missed appointments
and all vain escapes we praise
in songs and dance and poems
and creative pretences to permanence,
we draw our breaths with fire
and blood, rumble through the earth
with the passion of gods
with loud bells and talking drums
on their heels like kings, like men
unafraid of the memories we weave.

If Only
(For Oláìtán)

Yesterday, in a restless dream
Outside of my weary self, and
Under a blanket like a sour stream

Came, again, memories of you
At the end of a journey that bore
No hint of this sadness or two,

Carrying nothing but trepidation
Hiding in nine month's painful wait
And dread: delicate in fate's rotation.

Noon left as it came, with a darkening
Growth under our now joyless eyes
Ending May's promise in the reckoning

Twice unexpected, twice breaking, twice
Harrowing down into the marrows where
Evening tears prove impotent to revise.

Whenever the thought now returns
And futility slaps facts into sobriety
Yearning for what's gone just sorely burns.

In the beginning was the wary word.
That should have been left unheard.
Earth should wind itself back up into

Nicer outcomes for bearers of life,
Dangling softer pillows of creation
So oft grimly thrust like a blunt knife.

If These Were Written In Times Past

They would smell of rum, maybe wine
Of a pristine dance on brown keys that tapped,
Rasped in echoes across father's dusty lounge.

They would reek of innocence, shy lines
Of the toddler whose eyes lay only in the silence
laden trivia of books, and old record sleeves.

They might show relics of a hopeful child lie
Within a bulwark of rage in the silence of night,
Quiet, when adults slept, ears apart, still.

They would flee at the author's disgust
for past bustles, home noise and day jobs,
Useless rants that deter or fuel a budding muse.

But it wasn't written then, and so the past remains
In bits of old rum in even older flasks, and pains.

Bad Connections

Bàbá wrote to me
through a lover, often;
nested text messages
of varying capitalisation.

Night at the hostel,
memories beckoned from home
over known objections
that blurred warning signs.

The distance was never
enough to kill what
remained as the last link
between our sundering home

And contact showed then, at last,
shards of what we'd left unsaid, wisely;
what being away has brought
as painful value to appeasement.

Ex-ilé

What should one say
In defense of goodbyes?
A bird at rest on a burning tree.
A traveler stuck on a lost boat.
A leaf in the eye of the wind.

Hooked to earth we float
On the hope that stories
Themselves can bring life
To moments where reality fails,
Where time hides a scream.

And far away, all that was
Familiar crowds the air in colours
Of memory, regrets, loves,
Songs and faces, moments
That never come back the same.

So distance becomes the familiar,
And home now a journey
Through the many bodies I've lived;
Now is the road that winds them taut
Like the strap of a drum.

An Empty Town
March '20 in London

Half Cup is half-empty
Bread no longer much of a draw
When the aliens offer warning
Of their coming rave.

The earth seemed to notice;
I saw a flower bloom
On a tree, doves playing
With more abandon on Judd street

Than I remembered
When humans walked here
With a zest I recognised, though
Not any more happier than now…

As if to tell us who the real stranger
Is to whom the earth is host
For ravaging. To whom
Earth is forest weed for pruning.

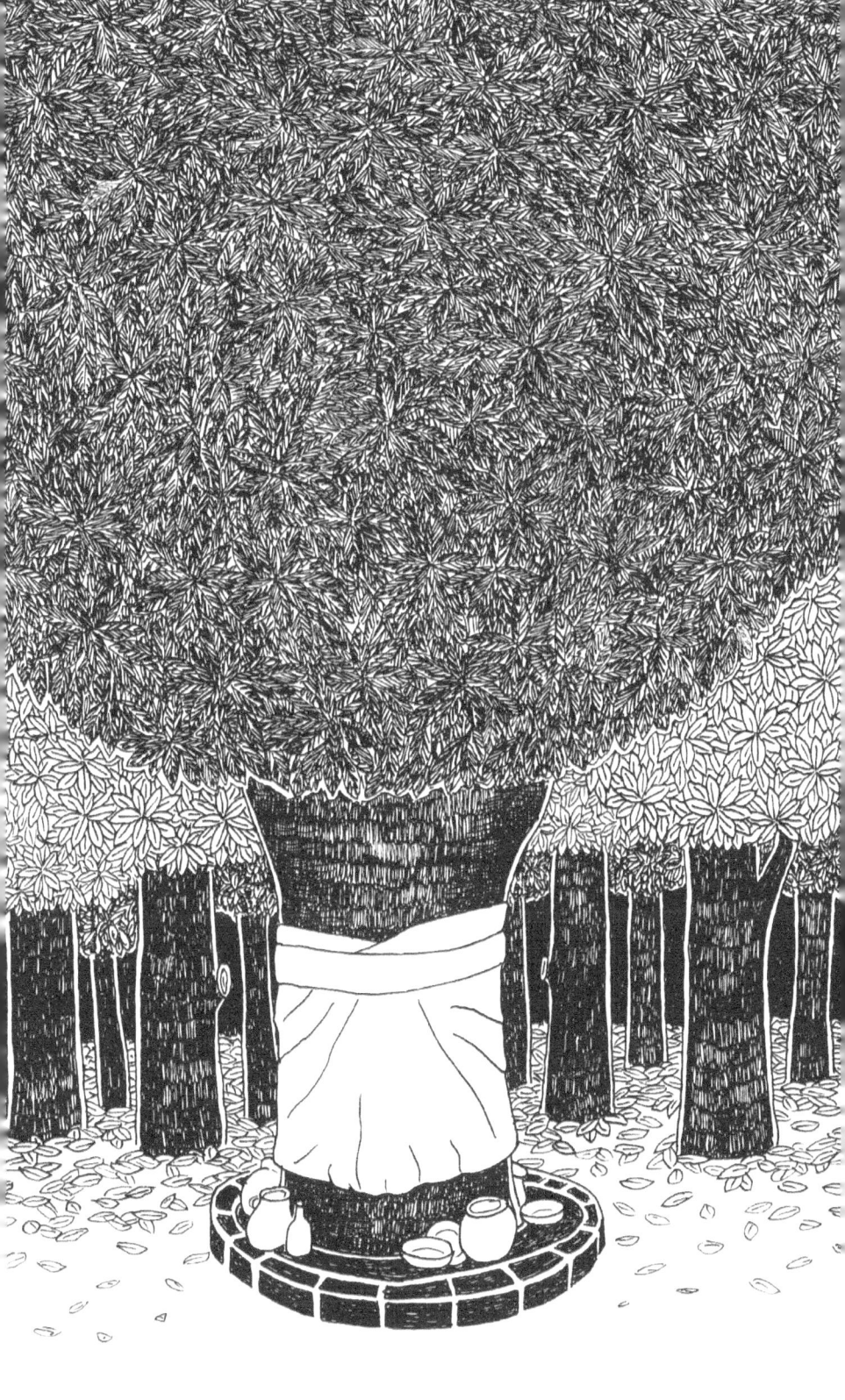

No Rolls at Waitrose

At Apocalypse,
We will lack food and drinks
And hugs and warmth.
We will greet each other
From a distance, head nods
And a smile, no hands stretched.
But we will lack no toilet rolls.

The aisles will be filled
With red grapes and sugar
And biscuits and ginger
Tea, and coffee, and hot cross buns.
Chantelle hands me two blades
Of lemongrass. "Good for the season.
Add a dash of honey and warm water."

But when the city goes numb
And the trains stop roaring
Underground — their noise reaching
Me on the third floor at Euston Road
I'll remember the evening when
The city chose the which holes to pet
In the winter of pestilent silence.

Quiet

Music beats dust pollens
Into petals, with a pulsing fear.
The horn of a highlife past
Waltz with the with silences
Of solitude, pierce the joke
Of herd immunity the Prime Minister
Asked the country to embrace.
Drums the white noises
Of the modern apocalypse
Into patterns that a conquered
People know from their dreams.
While Americans dance
To beats of the viral mall
And Brits pace around the streets
In tense bravado,
Guitar strums of the promised
Whimper of the world's end
Play to the tune of Auld Lang Syne.

RED

"Everyone is crying tears, but Láaróyè is crying blood."
— *Èṣù's praise poem*

Blood-Spangled Banner

In the Ezu River of bones and blood
The bodies sing with the reddened mud
Dirges of a lost country that never was,
Words that never came when they called
In the dead of the night, faced with gloom.

In the white of a flag, the bleeding soul
Of the moment wept blood near the gaping toll —
Ghosts of the nation's past haunting the cries
Their bodies made in that horrid night
Singing the words written to mock their hope.

In Oke's twenty-year neck is a hole. A stab,
Says the hasty report not yet run through the lab
Of truth or the fog of the moment's misdirections.
His blood seeps across the curfewed streets
Into the veins of a future weeping regrets.

On the streets, the marauders mark the ground
With the casings of their killing rounds
Picked up hurriedly to mask the proof
That the promises are vain that the leaders make;
That the land is still a butcher's slab.

Maximum Restraints
For the NPF, a month after.[4]

When met at night with the loud placards
That spilled rude venom of rage, shards

Of truth that pierced armour plates bought
With state funds, the cops said they fought

With maximum restraints; like the shells spilled
In blood and loss around the Lagos fields

Tell us nothing our bodies already know:
That lead doesn't mix well with blood like so,

That the selves now missing did not take a hike
Into the throng of fleeing feet and melt like

Ice into the concrete of the shrine where their gods
Chose to take their sacrifice with each searing nod.

That the lagoon did not just gnaw on young bones
In the marsh of that night; it also gulped their groans.

---

[4] On October 20, 2020, Nigerian soldiers opened fire on peaceful protesters at a toll gate in Lekki, Lagos, killing scores of people and wounding many. The state first denied its involvement, but in the next few weeks, the police grudgingly claimed responsibility, claiming the use of "maximum restraints" during the events. https://x.com/PoliceNG/status/1322079969397399552

As fright pushed resolve into its gaping throat,
They that couldn't swim were, in the next days, afloat.

So the horror we saw with our own weeping eyes
Of cops aiming guns at fleeing men are just a nice

Display of their night pageants — Hot blessings
From the black barrels of our benevolent kings?

What else is there to do but give thanks where due,
To the spirits from whom these farces accrue?

Soldiers in Lagos

Are answer to a question never posed
In Lagos or Warri or Ìbàdàn or Aba
As response to the fear of a viral load.

The koboko was never the pleas that Siri
Yelled over the slit broken ventilators
Or the choking of lungs already weary

From smoke, dust, chemicals, a fate
Decibels worse than death by a Wuhan guest.
Or one more boot on a broken face.

The rape threats, frog jumps — a parade of rot
For powerdrunk profligates on empty streets
Only bend to the trauma we almost forgot.

From when mothers' prayers began in turns
At the house fence for the child on an errand
To a nearby street, sustained until she returns

Whole, limbs intact, safe from the bloodlust
Of the state's reckless gimps on a rampage.
Not even time nor elections have brought results.

We are back here, virus-bound, to a state
Of surrender, to soulless dregs in camouflage,
With tears to the new badges of a reprobate.

Capel Celyn
Or How to Drown a Tongue[5]

Economics first, not thirst or memory
Of those disturbed from their bed of earth
Centuries long, tongues parched from words
That may never be spoken again. Violence.
Rub the salt of power in the sore of the dead;
Who cares for the stories that language encode —
The bits of ourselves left in the words ancestors spoke?
Under the lake of greed's dominant muscles
They remain, bones and tombstones as seasonal
Remnants of resistance reaching out in summertime
To touch the living, not just in Liverpool.

Or how is it, then, far away in the Savannah
That the thirst that nearly drowned a country
Has also burned down a library of memories?
Even here, in verse, complete capitulation stares
Back from where the same weapon trains itself
Like a reservoir to the valley of our native tongue.
Ọgbọ́n ọlọ́gbọ́n kìí jẹ́ ká pe àgbà ní wèrè[6] —

---

5   *Capel Celyn was a rural community in North Wales, in the Afon Tryweryn valley. It was, in 1965 before it was deliberately flooded by the British government to make way for a reservoir to supply water to Liverpool, one of the last places where Welsh was spoken as a first and only language.*
6   *Yorùbá proverb: "The possibility of borrowed wisdom is why we don't call adults crazy."*

Is relevant wisdom, where "Ogun àwítẹ́lẹ̀..[7]."
Fails to remedy the pain of dislocation,
And all that is left is vain resistance.

From Maung or Igbanke to Cymru or Hawaii,
The waters call to fishermen of memory, and song.
While we cannot always wait for dry summers
And random emergence of hidden fossils
The rhythms of paddles and the scent of roasts
Might bring more to the taste of tomorrow
Hiding under these fabrics of modern times.
It is for my own demise that I write a song;
It is for the village that the rhythm is sung —
Gaggles of foreign waters in a roiling monotone.

The valley is a hail of lies the radio blarres,
Or a rain of lead from a horde on a march
Loud in their thirst for blood where your tongues
Used to be. The waters cover a multitude.
The parches of soil do not respond when trod
By the ages, leaving only wisps of grass,
Silences across the field of bleeding syllables.

---

[7] *Yorùbá proverb, in full: "A war long foretold does not kill the cripple."*

On New Year's Eve

We forgot to move the clock
Forward to trick the kids
Of the slow passage of time;

Fake a cemetery peace for calm
While the village burns from the righteous
Pounding of world power blindness.

We eat, we trade smiles in the promise
That this silent evening breeze
Maps the gentle world they know;

We hide crumpled truths behind
The ears of exploding years
Already wearing its masks of hubris.

The Snob

"How'd you like living without
a threat of gun violence?"
I'd wanted to ask the Americans
Whose smile warmed my morning
On the way to the canteen
In blush glows beaming of a recent past
The things that might unite the passion
Of our familiar exiles.

From a distance, the news of home
And the idiocy of the government
And the violence of guns
And the hopelessness of youth.
Hit us here in the cocoon
Of the English sun, erratic still
But gentle on the mind
Suited for years to the sound of war
In the rattle of guns and the silence
Of deaf and well-dressed presidents.

Do I speak of America or Nigeria,
Los Angeles or Chibok? Kids punctured
Into bits by the rattles of our negligence?
Lagos or Chicago, gangs with government
Names or colours of ancient grievances?
Washington or Abuja — well ordered

Procession of statecraft, obscuring
Shades of deceit, betrayal, nonchalance.
Care only for what the pocket deserves?

Here, with nothing but knives to fear
When hunger and exuberance
Pushes bratty contentment to stupor,
We retire into the bottom of pint glasses
For the comfort of distance.

To A January 6th Friend.
For CL

In the safety of West African bombs
And lapses, under rulers with gators
For garb. In the silence of tombs.

The gag of practised leather boots
On the throat of the moment, shots
Fired in the night in white hot pursuits.

In the darkness of my own silence
Against what I know to be true and strange.
In the cesspool of noise across the fence.

Memories revive the hot speech bubbles
Of our flights; angry spits of rage.
Loud ramblings of Yankees' own troubles.

Bile at stranger topics I hadn't thought
I'd hear from a bosom friend, red eyes
And rote recalls of hate points, whatnot.

Worried about you and your demons;
Worried that you bought too much stake
In the boiling moss of your home's angry sons.

Scared that you were there in that wintery cage
In the harried throng that had turned blind
To reason and country, bound up in public rage

At the Capitol where the shame of the West
Was laid bare in its mud-addled soul,
Where sense died on a full-bloodied crest.

Wondering from my distance if perhaps reason
Had found you in my absence. Whether
Hope had set you free from your own prison.

Needing visual proof that the hubris of time
And country lore has tampered your angst
At windmills of your mind's wildest design.

No Wine in my Quarantine
To Nigerian English and a viral drought

Chords E and G, half-mute fumblings
Through the night that is long and dry jest,
And a fridge that is full, on which a leg rests.
There is hot food and plenty on which to dine
But there is no wine in my quarantine.

Zoom, they say, and other web lens
Bring the world near, stuck to their looms
With babbling tones, house party rooms
And emails that begin with "I hope you're fine."
Yet there's no wine in my quarantine.

I see the bridge out of my window, Nollywood
Astride the lagoon under the cover
Of dark, with boats awaiting rides of lovers
Eager to row through the dark herb of brine
And still no wine for my quarantine.

London is gone now, with its wry smiles, faces
Behind the veil of history's guilt and mood,
Drying up with the city's torso now stark nude.
I am here alone in the pretense to better times
But still no wine in my quarantine.

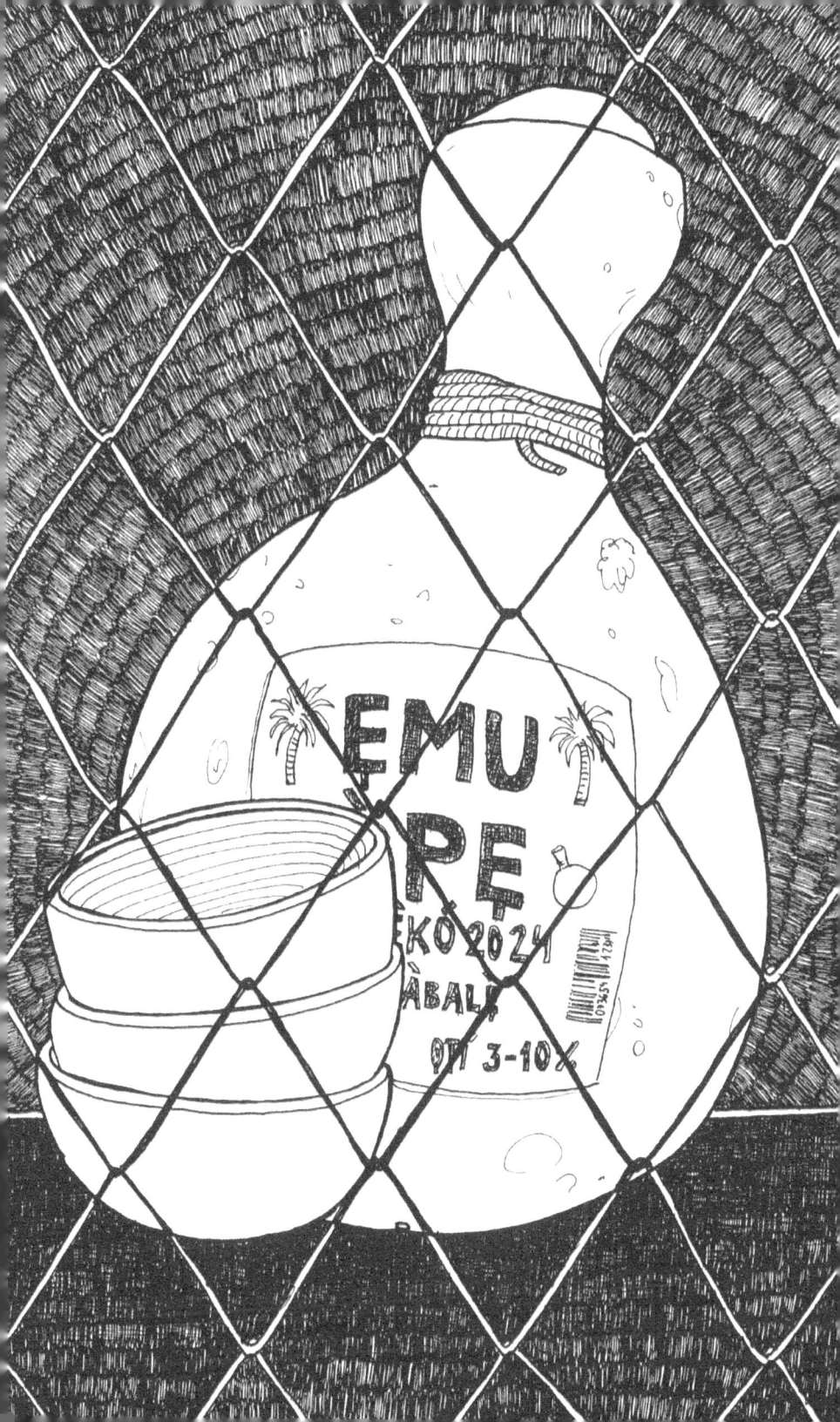

Sister visited last night, and in a distance
Wove our fears into jokes we shared as refrain
And hugs that could never be, lest we bring more pain
To the heart of those for whom we'd rather pine
Who brings no wine, though, to my quarantine.

Distance the taste of memories, the wine shop
Lay across the street far from the cravings; hence
Science, which reminds to stave in stoic silence,
Smile at the screen with a love that waits its time;
Smuggled into my quarantine, the taste of wine.

London is a Yorùbá Town
Written from a balcony at Google, overlooking King's Cross Station.

I

A river splits the town in two
In part, a stream of memories,
On one side, fossils and flowers
In the sand, on the other, a moment
That rhymes with history's children.
At the bank, worshippers stare
With gadgets in hand, swarming
Like votaries of a god.

There are huts many metres tall
That dot the village paths, harbours
Of lights poured deep into the sky.
The villagers gather at night
In street corners, over a glow
with meat and wine and grumbles
And ruckus of life and bodies
In sweat on a distant screen.

The gods, intemperate, battle out
Their discontent in a restless sky.
Not Zeus, Ṣàngó; Not Poseidon,
Ọṣun. Not Loki with the tricks, Èṣù

At the crossroads near St. Pancras.
Not the five market days in Ìrè
But tweed jackets and paper bags
Rushing home through quiet streets.

This *Town of the King*, as we once
Called it was never quite real
For us children. From Àkóbọ̀, magic
Seemed left in the question of how a town
Can exist beyond the clouds;
Beyond what the child's mind could tell
In the stories sworn to be true, where
Neighbours went and never returned.

Because heaven was too far off to draw
From the text the scriptures gave
In the imagery of its scribes,
Lands beyond the reach of the mind —
Beyond the scope of a pair of eyes
Looking up — filled in the rest with words
Before the books did the rest in lines
And lies in sweet nursery rhymes[8].

The Queen sits on a carved wood stool,
Horsetail of gold in one hand,
With beaded wrists holding a scepter of ivory
(A 'gift' from Admiral Rawson, it said

---

8   A popular childhood ditty chants to the aeroplane flying overhead to greet "Ìyá mi ẹlẹ́kọ" who left food insufficient for the child's hunger.

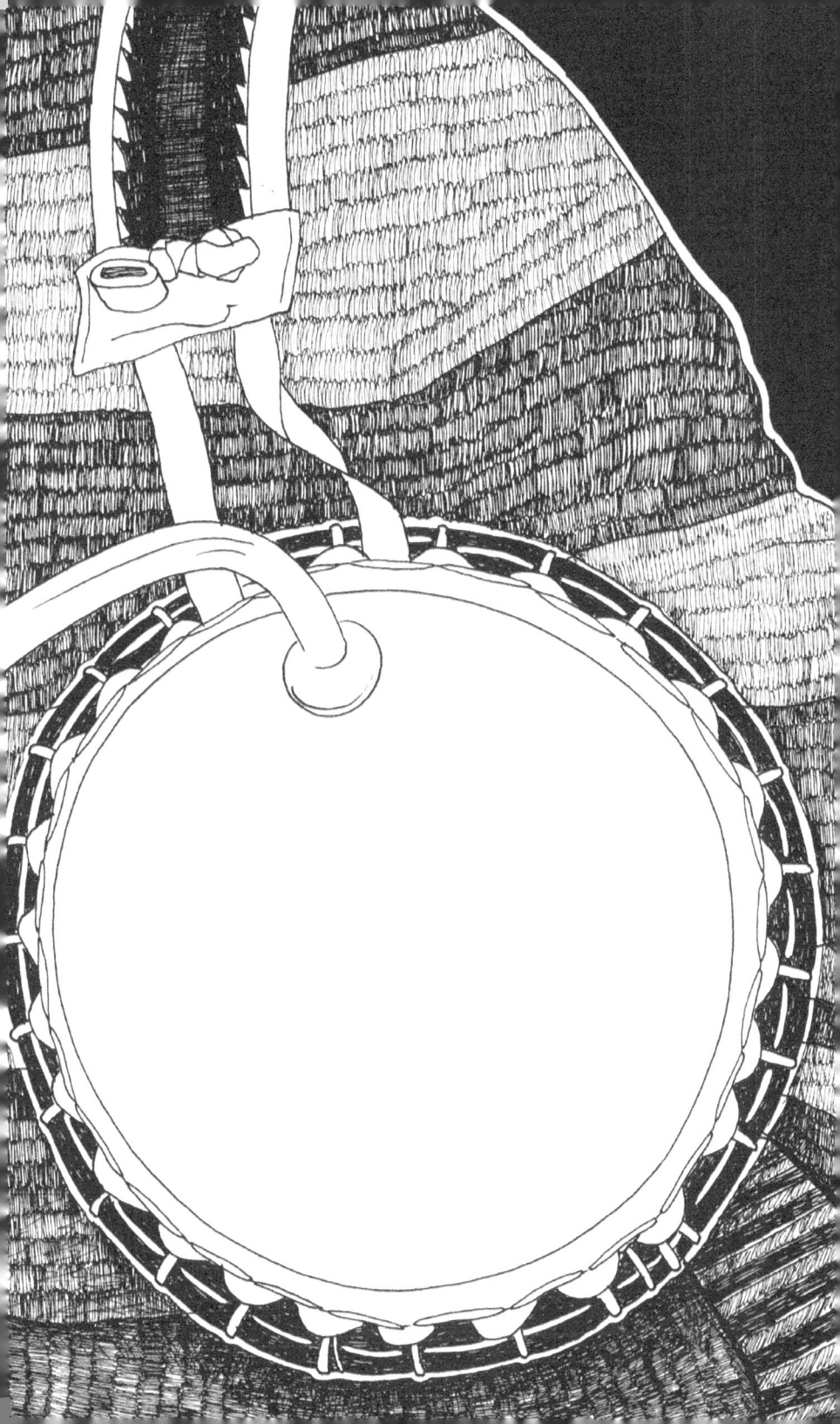

On the replica in a glass at the BM)
Whose white sparkles like ancient teeth.
She hails a fawning crowd gathered
For benediction of her spurious wave.

The Ọyọ́mèsì sit in Parliament,
In a circle, on the floor, throwing parrot eggs
At each other's faces in battle.
It is daylight here and the incantations,
In crisp British cadence, rasp to the cameras
Amidst the chaos. When the night comes,
They are out on the street rowdy as rain,
Wrapped in flowing gowns and soaked feet.

Destined for the British Library on Euston Rd,
Beaded too, with cowries on the spine,
Their words run poetry colours of indigo,
Wax-sealed for posterity with songs on the page.
I watch from afar, on foot, sometimes in a dream
And sometimes right there, talking drum
Under the armpit, beating the memories
Of the day's events into distant records.

II

Tí m bá dé London
Ma wá f'owó ọkọ̀ ránṣẹ́
Ọmọ pupa o
Jọ̀wọ́ mo fẹràn rẹ o

On the terrace up at Pancras Square, I sit,
God-like as the old women do at Olúmọ.
The city spreads like history in roof shapes
Across the light-suffused city bearing legs
And destination-bound pedestrians below.
I have sat like this by the ocean elsewhere
Watching ships come slowly in to dock,
Thinking about lies all travellers tell.

Oh how the country maps
The four old kingdom into one
over annual quarrels over land,
Women, power, and tradition.
Ifẹ is to the middle, where it all began;
A median between Ìbàdàn and Ekiti;
Òṣogbo is in the north perched across
A crossroads with Ọyọ́ in the line of vision.

Orí yéye ní Mògún[9], the many heads
On the ground around the London Tower
Now decomposed into the earth
Under our hundred tourists' feet
Belonged, like those of our king's foes,
To the many pets of fate's trickery.
The many victims of our civilization
Do not always fit the mind's design.

---

9 'Of the many heads littered at Mògún, many belong to the innocents' – a Yorùbá proverb.

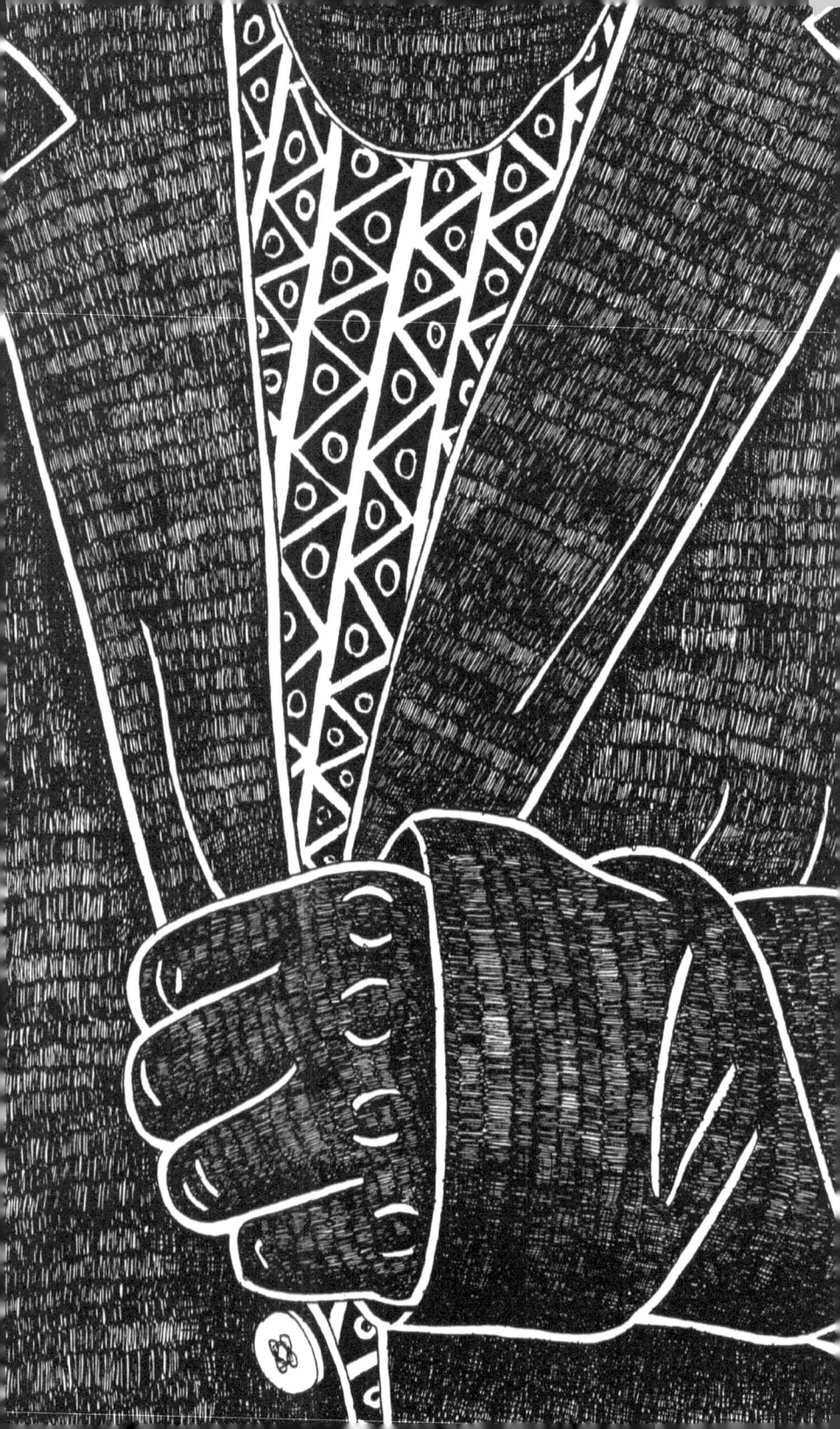

And the many histories that haunt —
Sarah Bonetta, Samuel Crowther,
Dami Taylor, Ṣadé Adú, John Bóyèga
— And the many whose record
Roil with the rivers roaring beneath
The bridges and its many city scars
Came back with the tonality of the drum.
Only the Queen's men refused to hear it.

Guns in hand at the city toll
In the night, with no warnings bells,
Royal infantrymen opened rapid fire
And the cry of a generation was silenced
Into the night with scant recoil.
I watched it all that October night
the princely chiefs in dead uniform,
and garbs of lies to keep the kingdom still.

III

Come and go, like January's rain
Once here, the other moment is gone.
Colour sometimes, clarity at another.
Surrenders us to the empiric vial.
Have we come back here only
As incarnates of our own withered past?

Our waist beads heavy from dancing,
Pen sticks scrawling back the moods

From which we have sought escape...
The language from where the castles
Keep us locked in a constant whirl,
Professes its impotence to our cause.

So we sing instead for the remnants
Of familiarity we find in the cold?
Olóòlù is at Covent Garden, floating
On a shovel, a Roman soldier adjacent,
Throwing swords at the feet of children
Happy for the freedoms that many seek.

Faraway from home, this town —
Half underground like dead ancestors
Trolling the warrens in search of rest —
Spreads thick and thin depending on where
The pubs are housed, shrines by the corners
Where the gut is worshipped.

The old empire lay in ruins now
Horsetail whips turned to protest icons
For by-elections where the brooms failed
To fool the voters. A sovereign
Splits his own land into weaker parts
And crowns each piece a new king.

The English Channel is the Ògùn River
Cutting through years of war and raid.
The Dahomeans paddle through in the night

Heading for the small town under the rock
Where the tongue has evolved slightly
Into a new language wrapped in song.

At the train station, a soft voice
From behind, in the phone argument
Calls to another in a tune
I recognize. "Mo ti sọ fún ẹ pé…"
And all the syllables arrange familiar
Colours from Ayẹ́yẹ́ to Yemẹtu.

Raindrops on corrugated roof
Of the mouth are heavy with rhythms
Of history, tone and song.
You cannot unhear it when it lands
On the ear, with all the warmth
Of its distant rhythms like gángan drums.

I know it. By the looks she gave me,
She knows that I know it too.
But I don't intrude on the conversation
Nor acknowledge more than the turn
Of the head already did. We belong
Here now, like firm branches to a tree.

IV

The cold does not always allow
For the colours of sányán, of ẹtù

Of àdìrẹ ẹlẹ́kọ and other energies
Of fabric experimentation,
To thrive under its heavy wrap
Of thick, wooly, tripes of conformity.

Human skins under animal skins,
Under nature under the industry
Of the modern age. We wrap
Ourselves in the safety of wool,
Where formality blends comfort
With acceptance, ropes on the neck.

What will kill us rents the air without
A sound. The priest, in the bus, stares
As the acolytes file in, sacrifices
In hand, in the small sheet they press
To the bleeping circle of the god's eye.
He holds the divination wheel to his chest.

On this Sunday morning ride, the voices
In the bus take the English rhythms
To task, like charmed verses chanted
In the morning without regard to neighbours'
Sleeping hour. The clothes they wear
Call for a nod I gave, but wasn't returned.

At Hackney, out of Sophie's flat one day
To get a piece of bread at the nearby
Store, the woman in glossy colours,

Dressed for church, loudly demanded
Of her daughter who had taken too much
Time to get ready. "Dá mi lóhùn…"

It caught me unawares, the two seconds
Arrest that kept me there, at the spot,
Unable to flee the glare of sudden
Recognition. Groceries in hand,
I returned into the house where other colours
Of Yorùbá memories soothed the morning.

"The Met Police wants more speakers
Of Nigerian languages in the force, Yorùbá,
Igbo…" the news was read to me, a fresh graduate.
To which the questions are neither just praise
To heavens for open doors, but wary thoughts
About what crimes had made this timely.

V

Ọpá Ọrànmíyàn is downtown, a clock on its ivory face
Beside the Parliament where the laws are made,
Written in parchment scrolls.
Alone, I divine my way home on the tablet
That glows knowledge and light and dust pixels.

The consonant clusters have survived
This incarnation of home: Rochester, Dartford,
Cockfoster, Watford, Kent. Oh Kent.

South London. The Jubilee Line, Peckham,
Where the plantains are ripe and cheap;
Edinburgh where the syllables run like gum.

Back at the Library, two brothers known
By the conversations they have in the middle
Of the cafeteria, in the language we share,
Draw my distant participant in a ritual
beside the ordering stand where potatoes
and syruppy beans stare back beside the gray soup

The tones wrap themselves around my ears
As a part of this verse that isn't mine,
Ìbejì voices ring of home in the crowded room.
Weave me in without asking, and with no reprieve
Than a nod on the escape, out, to a more British noise.

Home as lights

Glass pebbles green
And red and blue; disguised
Views through the oval window
Many miles up above, now low
Now approaching the tarmac
Aided again by a blank
Blanket of night.
Lagos, often, is lines and moving eyes.

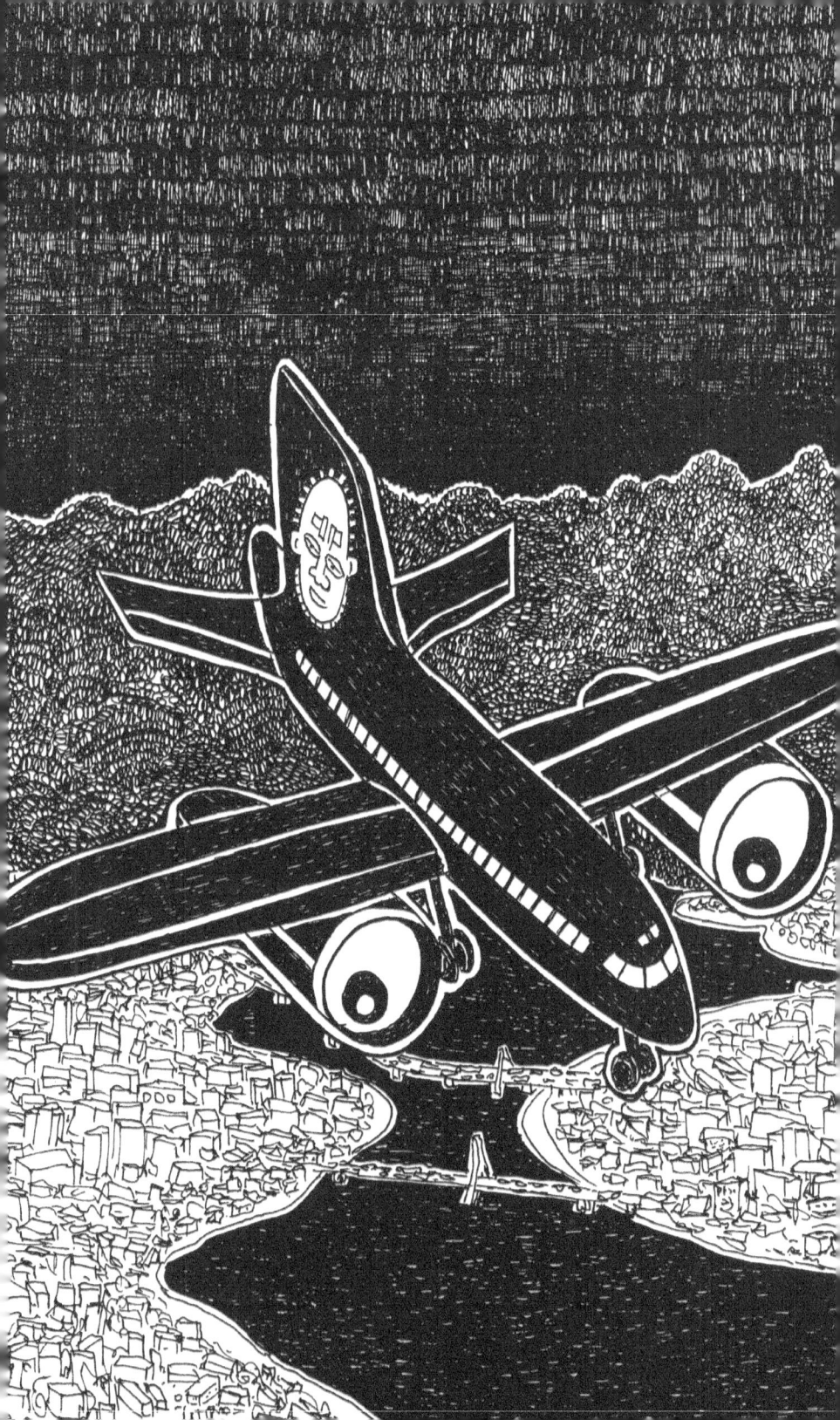

Acknowledgements

"Chat Call" was first published in *NTLitMag Issue* #7. April 2012.

"If Only" was first published in *Aké Review* 2016.

"Last Tweets" was first published in *Wreaths for a Wayfarer: An Anthology in honour of Pius Adésanmí* (February, 2020)

"A Linguist at Primark" was first published in the May 2020 issue of *Goodenough Magazine*

"Blood Spangled Banner" was published in *Sọ̀rọ̀ Sókè EndSARS Anthology* (February. 2022) Edited by Jumoke Verissimo and James Yeku

"Gone Innocence" was first published in Isele Magazine in July 2023.

Three later poems "Russell Square Station", "The Books Left Behind" and "Crowther's Dilemma" did not make it into the Nigerian edition of this collection, published by Masobe Books.

All changes to their earlier forms are minimal.

***

Thanks are due to Jídé Salawu, Benson Eluma, Chris Ogúnlọ́wọ̀, Yẹmí Adésànyà, Prof. Wọlé Ṣóyínká, and many friends and colleagues who read some of the poems in an earlier form.

To Moussa Kone for the drawings.

And to Olúwalóní who lets me bother her with practice read-outs at odd hours.

Appendix

From "Samuel Crowther
A Vocabulary of the Yoruba Language (1843)"

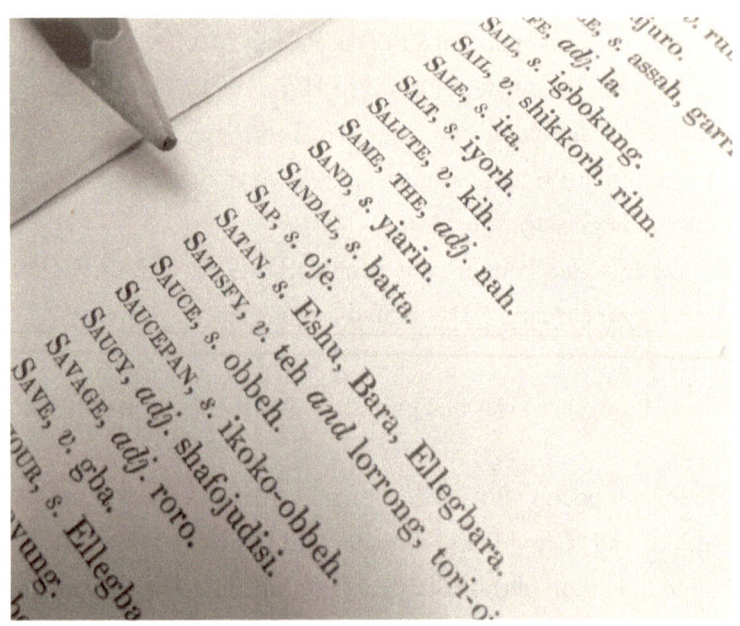

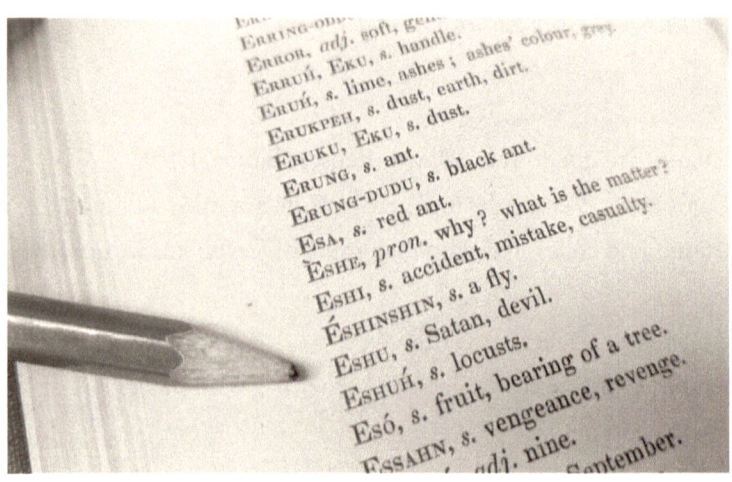

ro ninu ... -ping, n. igi ti o ṣeṣe hu.
la. Sapphire, n. okuta oniyebiye.
ipara. Sarcasm, n. ẹgàn, abukun.
Sarcastic, adj. pẹlu ẹgàn.
Sardine, n. ẹga kekere.
Sash, n. ọja, lawani; igi oju ferese.
n. Satan, n. eṣu, olori ọrun apadi.
Satanic, adj. ti eṣu, bi eṣu.

despite ... arankan, aikasi, ... dagba. ... i. ìparun,
ibinu. Development, n. idagba, ìhu,
... v.t. kò lí ẹrù, ja li ole. Deviate, v.i. yàna, yapa, ṣina.
... ireti nu, wà Deviation, n. iyà kuro lọna, iṣina.
non... ... Device, n. imọ iṣe, erọ, ọgbọn.
n. alagbu... Devil, n. eṣu.
m, n. iwa agbara, ìròrò. Devil-worship, n. isin eṣu.
n. eso, ajẹkẹhin onje. Devise, v.t. ṣerọ, gbimọ, humọ.
u, n. ibi ti a nlọ. Devoid, adj. alaini.
t, pinnu, kadara. Devolve, v.t. and i. kàn, ...
opin nkan tabi Devote, v.t. and i. ya ...
laini, kikọsilẹ. mimọ ...

... ọrun. Demented, ... n. iwa, ilò.
... Demented, adj. ṣiwere.
... mu irẹwẹsi Demijohn, n. ṣago.
Democracy, n. ijọba nibiti agbara wà lọwọ awọn enia.
... Democrat, n. ẹniti kò fẹ́ ọba.
iradara,... Demolish, v.t. run, bajẹ, fọ́.
didun, ayọ. Demolition, n. ibajẹ, rirun, ifọ́.
u, niparun. Demon, n. eṣu, iwin.
... i. rò, Demoniac, n. ẹlẹmi eṣu.
Demonstrate, v.t. and i. fi-hàn...
fi-ladi.
... iwolẹ Demonstration Demo...

About the Author

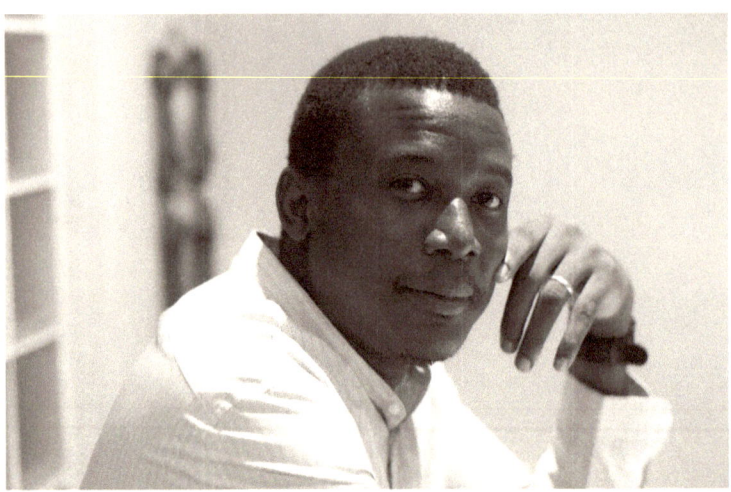

Kọ́lá Túbọ̀sún is a Nigerian writer and linguist, currently the Africa editor of *Best Literary Translations* anthology, published annually by Deep Vellum. His work has been published in *African Writer, Aké Review, Brittle Paper, International Literary Quarterly, PEN Transmissions, Enkare Review, Maple Tree Literary Supplement, Jalada, Popula, Saraba Magazine, World Literature Today,* etc. He has translated the works of Chimamanda Adichie, Haruki Murakami, Ngugi wa Thiong'o, Wole Soyinka, James Baldwin, Sarah Ladipo-Manyika, Cervantes, and others between English and Yorùbá. His work in language advocacy earned him the Premio Ostana Special Prize in Cuneo Italy in 2016. Read more at kolatubosun.com

Author's photo by Victor Adéwálé.

www.ingramcontent.com/pod-product-compliance
Lightning Source LLC
Chambersburg PA
CBHW031434210526
45464CB00005B/2193